BRITISH RAIL NORTHERN SCENE

A 1970s Railway Album

ANDY SPARKS

SUTTON PUBLISHING

First published in 2006 by
Sutton Publishing Limited · Phoenix Mill
Thrupp · Stroud · Gloucestershire · GL5 2BU

British Library Cataloguing in Publication Data
A catalogue record for this book is available from the
British Library.

ISBN 0-7509-4258-4

Viewed from Manchester Victoria's derelict
Platform 2 a Class 504 electric unit is seen arriving
with a service from Bury Bolton Street on a
winter's morning in 1979.

Typeset in 10/12 pt Novarese Bk.
Typesetting and origination by
Sutton Publishing Limited.
Printed and bound in England by
J.H. Haynes & Co. Ltd, Sparkford.

Contents

No. 304 018 leaves Manchester Piccadilly with an afternoon suburban train, summer 1978.

Whistle blower – Manchester Victoria, July 1978. This railway employee has his eye on the ticket barrier to check for any late passengers. If there are none he will blow his whistle so that the driver and guard of the Bury electric on Platform 5 can clearly hear him. This man would probably have had long railway service; thirty years would have taken him back to LMS days, fifty years almost to L&Y days. It is interesting to note that the billboards in the foreground advertise jobs in the commercial/professional sectors; at the time railway industry employment opportunities were not as well advertised as they are today.

Introduction

Born in 1958, I was old enough to witness the final years of BR steam, but unfortunately not to photograph it. Turning the pages of magazines and library books filled with stunning end-of-steam photographs, I – like so many other people – felt the opportunity to emulate such fine work had passed me by.

As a young train spotter during the early 1970s while roaming my part of the North – an area covering North Wales to Stoke-on-Trent in the south, east to Skipton and north to Carlisle: the North-West – I realised that very little had changed since my photographic heroes (Colin T. Gifford, Eric Treacy) created their evocative masterpieces. Except for the steam locomotive, the key elements – buildings, methods of operation, permanent way, people, signalling and trains – that made their photographs special still existed. Even as a thirteen-year-old I knew that the economic, political and social changes that were beginning to have a significant effect on daily life would eventually impact on the railways. If I waited for too long it was likely that my opportunity to emulate others would be lost forever.

A second-hand FED camera with several rolls of Kodak Tri X film – my fourteenth birthday present – was the catalyst that made the creation of this book possible. Shortly afterwards the rail scene did begin to change fundamentally and an eight-year quest began to record this largely unrecognised period in railway history. Better cameras, a Zorki 4 and Pentax SP1000, along with an improving photographic ability allowed me to capture the scene in my own special way. However, limited funds at the time meant that it was not until 2004/5 with a reawakened interest in railways and an improved disposable income that many of the images were reproduced on photographic paper. This finally revealed their historic, nostalgic, social and in a number of cases artistic value, prompting the creation of this book.

My words and pictures are intended to provide an enjoyable and thought-provoking journey through a period in railway history when a great deal of what had remained the same for generations was swept away by the decade of change – the 1970s.

Andy Sparks

Wigan Wallgate, November 1972. Today's railwayana collectors would love to get their hands on these delights, many of which were shortly destined for the skip. Few people, if any, would have imagined that a British Railways totem could command a four-figure sum in the twenty-first century.

Windermere station, Good Friday 1975, and the large platform clock tells us it is 7 minutes past 12 as a Class 108 two-car unit prepares to depart for Oxenholme. This station was the Furness Railway's number-one gateway to the Lakes, built to last with a full complement of facilities to serve the packed trains of day-trippers and holiday-makers that came from far and wide. Unfortunately there are telltale signs in this photograph that its days were numbered – the roof glass has been removed and there is just one platform in use. Eventually Booth's Supermarkets would rescue the station from oblivion, making it part of their Windermere outlet.

CHAPTER ONE

Station to Station

The 1970s was the last decade to sample the atmosphere and trappings of steam-age railway station life. The North-West was rich in stations, small, medium and large still retaining their proud, if a little threadbare, vestiges of a bygone age. Their architecture, facilities and people all combined to create an interesting mix which in many cases had little changed for decades. But 1970s modernisation, neglect, rationalisation and social change would spell the end of these wonderful time capsules full of delights.

ARCHITECTURE

The North-West's railway station history can be traced back to the pioneering days of the Liverpool and Manchester Railway, and in virtually every case since those early days stations were built to reflect the affluence and importance of the owning railway company (actual or perceived). They were the company's shopfront as well as the gateway to the cities, towns and villages they served.

Examples of all architectural styles, from Georgian, for example Manchester's Liverpool Road (the oldest railway station in the world), through to the 1960s modernism of Manchester Oxford Road, have been employed to create the right impression to clients – commercial, industrial and also the travelling public. In general, stations excelled in achieving their goal, but sadly by the 1970s basic accountancy principles made it clear that income would not cover the stations' spiralling maintenance and repair costs, making them liabilities rather than assets. 'Deferred maintenance' over many years meant that ageing brickwork, canopies, decoration, drainage, floors, roofing and utilities were beginning to become unsafe. Stations were also not in keeping with the travelling public's rising expectations. The public wanted modern, clean, bright, quality environments, and the bulk of the North-West's stations did not fulfil these criteria. British Rail's limited resources and vision sadly meant that the bulldozer, along with the scrap man, were the authority's answer to the problem. Sadly there was little respect for our heritage at the time and many gems were lost, with many canopies, train sheds, station buildings and platform furniture indiscriminately reduced to rubble by the end of the 1970s.

Thankfully several notables did survive their 1970s stay of execution into the more enlightened decades that followed: Carnforth was restored to its *Brief Encounter* glory, the Liverpool Exchange (closed 1977) frontage became part of an office complex, Manchester Central (closed 1969) is now the splendid G-Mex Exhibition Centre, and Manchester Victoria's redundant expanses were given over to the Nynex/MEN Arena and Metrolink, while others were sympathetically incorporated into shops or offices.

Today many of those stations that survived the 1970s are enjoying a renaissance through restoration, and good property management is making them once again the pride of the North-West.

FACILITIES

From the smallest to the largest stations, the comprehensive facilities bestowed on them by successive railway companies generally remained intact into the 1970s. Like the buildings that housed them, lack of investment and neglect had frozen them in another age. Modern commercial, economic and social realities meant that British Rail's management could not ignore the situation any longer. The facilities that were affected included:

Booking Offices: Cost-cutting Paytrains enabled booking offices to be closed at smaller railway stations throughout the North-West.

Refreshment Rooms (Buffet/Cafeteria): Today, with the exception of Hellifield and Stalybridge, these can only be found on the North-West's larger railway stations. Until the late 1970s they were to be found on the platforms of many of the area's medium-sized stations (especially junctions), providing a welcome respite for passengers, local people, railway staff and of course spotters. Station cutbacks, increased costs and falling revenue finally took their toll on this once common part of the North-West rail scene, and by the end of the decade most had become boarded-up rooms or had been demolished.

Clocks: Virtually every station had a timepiece, often a huge Victorian mechanical masterpiece which would today be the pride of any antique or railwayana collector's collection. Most hung from the cast-ironwork of canopy supports or on station walls, and the loss of many of these mounting points to the demolition man meant that the clocks had a similar fate. By the end of the '70s they were a rare beast and passengers had to rely on their watches or simply guess the time.

Information Offices: Most medium and large stations still retained these rooms where holiday train and Merrymaker information could be obtained. Train times could be sought, and ferry, seat and sleeper berth reservations could be made. Handbills, seducing the enthusiast into rail-borne adventures far and wide, could also be found in these special rooms, being neatly presented in hardwood-framed glass display units. Station cutbacks and modernisation made these places a rarity, which are now looked back on with nostalgia by many enthusiasts.

Kiosks: Newsagents, sweetshops and tobacconists could also be found on most medium to large stations; today only the largest and most important stations provide these facilities. The small kiosk, run by a friendly attendant, so long a feature of North-West stations, began to disappear from the very start of the 1970s. Increased rent and labour costs along with reducing sales gradually made them another victim of the 1970s world of change.

Left Luggage: Here travellers could leave luggage while breaking a journey, send luggage in advance (popular for holiday destinations) and collect lost property. By the end of the 1970s these facilities were also becoming few and far between, and today are a thing of the past. Perhaps this is only to be expected in our terrorism-conscious world in which unattended luggage is looked on with extreme suspicion.

Lighting: Lack of investment meant that gas and oil lighting at a surprising number of the North-West's railway stations lasted well into the 1970s – far longer than in the streets that surrounded them. Where electric lights existed, their effectiveness was undermined by grimy fittings. In all cases they were interesting period pieces that were swept away in great numbers during the mid-1970s. Their functional street lamp-style replacements were a vast improvement in candle power terms but a poor substitute aesthetically or atmospherically.

Payphones: By the 1970s increasing affluence had brought widespread telephone ownership throughout the North-West. As a result, people wanted to make use of the phone system far more than ever before. This also applied when they were travelling – not unlike in today's mobile phone-dominated world – and at the time the only way to satisfy this demand was by installing extra payphones, especially at railway stations. The mechanical wall-mounted 2p, 5p and 10p-operated payphone became an indispensable facility for the travelling public – both young and

Ringing home – Manchester Victoria, summer 1979. It's the school holidays and the little girl is on her way to Blackpool with her grandparents. Grandad has been given the job of looking after the luggage and his granddaughter while his wife uses the payphone. During a moment of distraction – watching his wife trying to get the two bob into the slot – the little girl takes the opportunity to wander off. Only grandmother's quick thinking – asking the little girl to speak on the phone – saves the day.

old – and could be seen within the confines of virtually every North-West railway station. Demand for them often meant that they were provided in close proximity to each other, the competing noise from three or four conversations taking place at once making their use sometimes fraught. Despite their popularity, by the 1980s their heyday was over, and widespread vandalism and later the mobile phone would undermine their status. Thirty years on the payphone is virtually redundant – something that once would have been hard to imagine.

Seats: During the 1970s the need for somewhere to sit was readily fulfilled by a wide choice of comfortable seats, many of which had provided support for generations of weary rail travellers. Like station buildings, you could make a fairly accurate guess at the age of a bench by looking at its design. Heavy Victorian wooden or cast-iron construction, Edwardian wrought-iron and wood construction, and 1930s/40s Art Deco featured along with the more basic modern designs of 1950s/60s/70s British Railways. A bench's railway company provenance could also be easily determined from a quick glance, with the Furness Railway, L&Y, LMS and LNWR for example all having their own designs. Whatever their age and design, benches generally had one thing in common – comfort – especially those leather- or moquette-clad versions in waiting rooms. With the rationalisation of station facilities during the 1970s this largely ignored part of our railway heritage was consigned in large numbers to the bonfire, and today you are lucky to find a bench to sit on at any North-West railway station.

Signs: Cast iron and enamel signs abounded around the North-West's railway stations during the first half of the 1970s. Pre-Grouping and pre-nationalisation examples, however, were swamped by the British Railways variant identifying stations and station facilities. The 1970s facilities cull meant that sign numbers were cut drastically, and those that remained quickly succumbed to the introduction of modern black-on-white signage. The amount of signs that were consigned to the scrap skip would make any railwayana collector weep; those that survived now command amazingly high prices.

Toilets and Washrooms: Perhaps not the most pleasant of subjects to include within this chapter, toilets and washrooms are however an important part of the story. Until the 1970s virtually every North-West railway station had toilet facilities and the larger ones were augmented by adjacent well-appointed (if a little worn) washrooms. Cubicles with heavy-duty coin-operated brass locks and chain-activated cisterns amid chipped, but well-presented, enamel washbasins were typical. Gents' toilets had the addition of urinals often in gleaming porcelain bearing the name of Armitage or Shanks flushed by water piped through highly polished copper pipes. Unfortunately the growing trend towards vandalism and cutbacks first brought neglect followed by closure, and then demolition of these sanitorial masterpieces as the 1970s unfolded. Those facilities that remained were 'modernised' using the most basic of décor and fittings that soon became shabby, unlike those they had replaced which had stood the test of a very long time.

Waiting Rooms: First Class, General and Ladies' waiting rooms could still be found on many of the North-West's railway stations during the early 1970s. Like the station toilets, they were a lasting credit to the railway companies who provided them for the benefit of their valued passengers. These cosy refuges would sadly suffer a similar fate. Those stations that were lucky enough to retain a waiting room, instead of receiving a bus shelter-style replacement, had the 'modernisation' treatment, which amounted to gloss-painted walls and a one-bar electric heater.

Vending Machines: To supplement or as a substitute for the station kiosks and refreshment rooms, the mechanical vending machines had become increasingly popular. By the 1970s it was possible to purchase chocolate, cigarettes, drinks, nametags, photographs, sandwiches, sweets and your weight from these often quite splendidly presented machines. They could often be seen close to their GPO counterparts (the payphone). Mechanical malfunctioning was typical – a block of chocolate could often be supplied via a half-opening drawer or a steaming hot drink could be delivered without a cup. 1970s rationalisation meant that unattended machines were prone to vandalism, robbery and neglect. Empty and wrecked machines were not what the passenger or vending machine company wanted; the only solution was to remove them from all but the larger stations.

PEOPLE

Railway stations are great places to watch people going places, at work, passing the time of day, meeting or saying goodbye.

During the 1970s station life was noticeably beginning to change as new social and economic influences began to have an impact on the people of the North-West.

You can see in these photographs that people still dressed their age rather than how they felt, making them look older than they perhaps were. However, there are also the first indications that today's easy, younger-looking way of dressing was on its way. 'Sensible' dress codes that had remained appropriate for 'milestone' ages between 30 and 70 started to disappear, especially at the younger end of the spectrum.

Also noticeable is the dress of station staff, which fell into three distinct categories: steam age typically worn by older employees; one that represented the low morale generated by the cutbacks and industrial strife of the time; and occasionally smart modern British Rail.

By far the biggest challenge to the status quo of station life came from the motorcar. By the 1970s mass car ownership had arrived, and there were few families without access to a British Leyland, Ford, Hillman, Vauxhall or foreign-made vehicle. For day trips, holidays, going shopping or to work, public transport was no longer the only option and it began to show on station platforms – they became much less populated.

Even the quickening demise of the traditionally large-scale employers such as engineering, manufacturing and mills had an effect on station usage. Annual works shutdowns (Wakes Week) had for generations created mass exoduses from towns around the North-West and these were coming to an end. Only the older generation kept the tradition of taking holidays at these times.

The disappearing old industries tended to be located close to railway stations, unlike the new employment providers. As a result, workers had no alternative but to turn their backs on travelling by train to work. Stations that ultimately succumbed to this trend included Miles Platting, Park and Pendleton.

During the 1970s North-West railway stations were in a no-win situation, having to endure deferred maintenance, reduced facilities and staffing cuts. The resulting tired, barren stations, along with the convenience of the motorcar, drove people away in large numbers, which perpetuated the downward spiral. It was only Local Government support, the success of InterCity services and the continuation of mail and parcels services that helped many stations through this difficult period.

Today local and long-distance rail travel in the North-West is buoyant; the area's railway stations are now being properly cared for and managed. It is ironic that this reversal of fortune has been largely generated by twenty-first-century travellers' desire to avoid today's heavily congested roads.

A Rock Ferry-bound Metro Cammell two-car unit prepares to leave Chester. This train would connect with Merseyrail-operated Class 503 electric trains for Liverpool and Wirral destinations. Today Merseyrail Class 507 and 508 electrics now serve Chester, making the Rock Ferry diesel service redundant. While first-generation DMUs no longer grace Chester, it is still possible to re-create this photo using modern units as the Victorian station remains largely unchanged from this summer 1979 view.

Glossop station, May 1978. Today this part of the station forms the entrance to a Co-op supermarket. While the operational station was reduced in size by 50 per cent, the change of use ensured this fine piece of architecture had a secure future.

Manchester Exchange station approach, February 1974. Despite the station being closed for five years, British Rail billboards were clearly in evidence. The Altrincham Interchange advertisement was an indication of things to come – the 1970s desire to establish an integrated transport system at important locations. Thirty years later the concept has not yet been fully achieved, though Altrincham remains one of the most successful examples with Metrolink, heavy rail and buses sharing the confines of the Interchange. The special offers promoted by the Co-op, Sealink and British Rail's 'Fair Deals' make interesting reading. The young girls are obviously not too perturbed about the rain as they head into the city centre, probably for a spot of window-shopping. The cars that can be seen parked on the station approach extend right into the station, which became a car park after its closure. The tall chimney in the background belonged to the now-closed Boddington's Brewery.

Through the bars – Bury Bolton Street station, winter 1977. A pair of Class 504 EMUs prepare to depart with a train bound for Manchester Victoria. At the time Bury's interchange was in its early stages of development, and this station's days were numbered, with dereliction followed by demolition thought to be in prospect. However, today it is still possible to recreate this photograph, with just one main difference – locomotive-hauled trains (including Black Fives, Pacifics and heritage diesels) have replaced the 504s. The station is now the headquarters and operating hub of the modern East Lancashire Railway. I wonder if the Mk 10 Jaguar, URN 679, still exists.

Stalybridge, winter 1974. A Class 100 unit waits with the Stockport-bound Paytrain. In this photograph the extent of the station's heavy glass canopies can clearly be seen. These structures became increasingly unsafe during the 1970s because of 'deferred maintenance'; demolition was the easiest/cheapest solution to the problem.

Stalybridge station shortly after a summer downpour, August 1973. The Class 104 DMU has just arrived with the 17.03 SX stopping train from Manchester Victoria.

Liverpool Lime Street, July 1979. A Manchester (via Warrington Central) service leaves a trail of fumes behind it as it passes a Newcastle-upon-Tyne train. The practice of leaving first-generation engines ticking over in the station created a very unhealthy carbon monoxide-filled environment which can be clearly seen in the photograph. Also of interest are the plastic vending machine cup and the mail trolleys neatly lined up along the middle of the platform.

Summertime gloom – Manchester Victoria, July 1977. In some cases over one hundred years of pollution from the North-West's domestic and industrial chimneys had by the 1970s left its stations very dark and dismal, even on the brightest of days. The move towards a cleaner environment got under way during the late 1970s. However, it has taken nearly thirty years to really make a difference and it is only now that brightness and cleanliness are common to the large majority of the area's railway stations.

Steam heat – Piccadilly, April 1978. Steam escaping from the coaches of the Harwich Boat Train appears a little incongruous in the modern 1970s environment of Manchester Piccadilly. The leak would undermine the efficiency of the train's heating system during its long journey to the east coast.

This photograph was taken at Stalybridge station during the winter of 1974. It was used in my CSE Art portfolio (Egerton Park Secondary Modern, Denton, 1975). I christened it 'Industry Personified'. The mill chimneys, gas lamp and the pollution-laden skies are long gone. I wonder what today's sixteen-year-olds would produce to illustrate this title.

Tail lamps, Manchester Victoria, July 1975. There was always a stock of oil lamps on hand for the station's many trains. Note the clever use of a pallet and trolley for easy movement around the station.

Below: Tending the lamps, August 1979. Despite Manchester Piccadilly being one the most modern stations in the North-West it still used oil lamps as buffer stop marker lights. Today these lamps have been replaced with large, unmistakable electric-powered red warning lamps – far safer but much less interesting.

Opposite: At least three pictures in one! The lady is treating herself to a bar of chocolate from one of those vending machines with 'drawers' that sometimes did not open fully, leaving the chocolate frustratingly half in and half out of the machine. The plaque, now long gone, marked the opening of the Woodhead Tunnel and the billboard displays one of the *Manchester Evening News'* many eye-catching adverts, a feature of stations in the 1970s.

WOODHEAD NEW TUNNEL

LENGTH 3 MILES 66 YARDS

OPENED BY

THE RT. HON. ALAN LENNOX-BOYD P.C. M.P.

MINISTER OF TRANSPORT AND CIVIL AVIATION

THURSDAY 3RD JUNE 1954

SHOULDN'T YOU
BE READING
MORE THAN JUST
POSTERS?

Order your Manchester Evening News

1

Nestlé

CONFECTIONERY

Star performer – Manchester Victoria, summer 1979. This lady obviously enjoys life and provides her customers with that vital ingredient – good humour and friendliness. At all of the North-West's major railway stations boxes of chocolates for the wife, girlfriend or mother, sweets, chewing gum, pipe tobacco and cigarettes (including 1970s favourites such as No. 6, Park Drive and Woodbines) could be readily obtained from these handy little shops. Today they have all been swept away and at the few stations that still have places to buy something for the journey they are far less friendly places, corporate uniformity and commercial pressures having stifled the personal touch.

Payphones and photo booth – Manchester Victoria, August 1978. These two ladies who have more than one generation between them are using the station's payphones. A common and well-used feature of 1970s railway stations, today they have almost disappeared, the convenience of mobile phones having made them virtually redundant. Photo booths, however, are still with us; our new world requires photo identification for so many things, making them a necessary part of life. Today the cost of using a booth would be at least £3, an inflation factor of ten times the 1979 price of 30p.

Heading home – Stalybridge, winter 1974. This lady makes her way out of the gloom of the glazed brick-lined subway where she will board the Paytrain bound for Guide Bridge, Denton, Reddish South and Stockport. Today this lady would be an easy target for a mugger: her handbag and shopping bag could easily be snatched. This photograph clearly shows how carefree people once were.

Ablutions. This gentleman is about to make use of the free Lancashire and Yorkshire Railway facilities at Manchester Victoria during August 1979. The spacious tiled Art Nouveau toilets and washrooms had worn well over the years and provided a welcome respite for the traveller, local trader and passer-by. Today only major stations such as Manchester Piccadilly have such comprehensive facilities, and there is now a continental-style fee to use them.

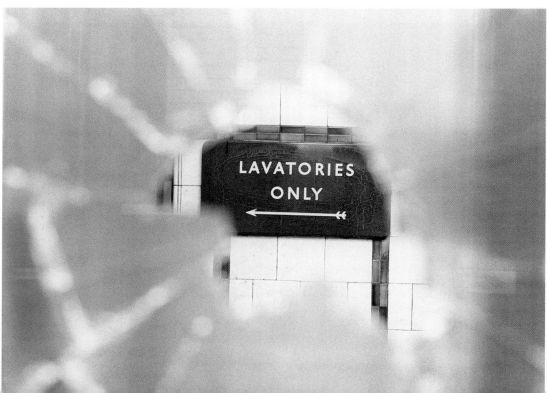

Time for a break – Manchester Victoria, August 1979. This couple, viewed through the mirror of the photo booth, make use of the side counter of a station kiosk while sampling the delights of the drinks vending machine. Nearby can be seen a Nestlé's chocolate vending machine and large-capacity weighing machine.

During the 1970s station cleanliness was not as well-managed as it is today. The steel dustbins (then a commonplace part of domestic life) and boxes tucked out of sight behind a platform end building provided the collection point for Platforms 5 and 6 at Manchester Victoria, May 1978. Like the dustbins, the 'Stera' (sterilised milk) bottles are now a rarity. Despite the unusual taste of their contents, they were popular for adding to tea and coffee.

Manchester Victoria, August 1979. Husband and wife walk in step towards the taxi rank on the final stage of their journey home after their annual seaside 'Wakes Week' holiday.

Taxi or bus? – A mother checks her purse to see if she has enough money left for a taxi ride home after she and her family have got off a summer Saturday train from North Wales. Her alternative would be to take the SELNEC Central 203 bus which terminated at the station. Despite it being the height of summer, the mother has got her headscarf on. She was probably trying to make her special holiday perm last a little longer in the damp Manchester weather.

A word in your ear – Guide Bridge, 1979. The incoming Class 506, M59403M, bound for Hadfield, goes unnoticed by this couple. What the lady has to say is obviously far more important. It is interesting to note that despite it being a hot July afternoon she has still got her sensible overcoat and heavy stockings on, her comfortable-looking white sandals being the only concession to the summer season.

Radcliffe station on a wet Saturday afternoon, July 1979. Passengers make full use of the suburban-pattern slam doors of the Bury-bound Class 504 unit, which allowed short stopping times at the closely spaced stations along the route.

Going on holiday – Manchester Victoria, July 1977. These lucky people are taking a break on the station concourse bench before heading towards Platform 11 for the train to their North Wales holiday resort. There is no risk of their cases bursting open en route, the heavy-duty supplementary straps will see to that. The seated lady has her holiday sandals on and her newly set hair rollers protected by a tightly tied headscarf – she obviously wants her hair to look its best on the first night at the digs. It looks as if the lady who is standing is not with the group and has been given the job of looking after the cases while her husband has gone to check up on train times. The gentleman, complete with well-polished shoes, at the end of the bench appears to be lightly laden, indicating he is on a day trip. His packet of raisins will provide sustenance on the journey and was probably purchased from the adjacent Finlay's kiosk. The hardwood L&Y booking windows can be seen in the background. Window No. 5's sign indicates that tickets for destinations beginning with L to Z plus Blackpool and Southport can be purchased there, which enabled queuing on busy days to be kept to a minimum.

Inter-City arrival – Manchester Victoria, May 1978. On yet another wet Manchester day a Class 47-hauled Liverpool–Newcastle train draws into Platform 12 with a rake of MkII air-conditioned stock. The wet platform shows that the station roof had seen better days; the waiting passengers would no doubt have been pleased that their train was on time.

Summer Saturday, Manchester Victoria, 1976. No. 25093 waits for its next station pilot duty while the Class 115 unit waits to depart on a Southport service. The young lad sitting on a suitcase talking to his dad is no doubt eager to climb aboard the Blackpool train shortly to arrive on Platform 12.

A last-minute passenger shouts back to the ticket barrier, 'Is this the one for Glossop?' Manchester Piccadilly, July 1978.

All change 1 – Oxenholme, July 1973. Passengers leaving the comparative luxury of an Anglo-Scottish Inter-City train head for the Kendal/Windermere Shuttle. By the 1970s the days of through loco-hauled trains to Windermere such as the 'Lakes Express' were history. However, a run round facility remained at Windermere for Merrymaker excursions and permanent way/maintenance trains. These 1970s passengers had to be satisfied with the class 108 unit; at least their connecting train's timings did not require a lengthy wait at the draughty Furness Railway-built Oxenholme station. Today second-generation units working through from such places as Manchester Airport serve Windermere branch line, which now also benefits from brand-new permanent way. Privatisation has brought positive initiatives which would have been inconceivable in the 1970s.

All change 2 – Kirkham, August 1977. These passengers who have just arrived off the London Euston to Blackpool North train climb aboard the St Annes/Blackpool South service provided by a Cravens 105 unit. The popularity of these Fylde destinations with both holiday-makers and locals ensured that this route remained open despite the closure of surrounding routes and stations – Blackpool Central and Fleetwood, for example – during the 1960s. Kirkham station has remained largely intact, its junction status ensuring it survived through the 1970s bulldozer revolution.

Ticket barrier 1 – Manchester Piccadilly, July 1978. As there is no train in Platform 3 the attendant is keeping his barrier closed. Piccadilly had a barrier for each of its bay platforms, which ensured better passenger control and work for everyone.

Opposite: Ticket barriers 2 and 3 – Manchester Victoria, July 1979. These ticket barriers are typical of those that featured at every medium and large railway station in the North-West until the 1970s, when an 'open station' policy began to be adopted. Lack of passenger control and 'revenue protection' resulted, and today personnel are beginning to be introduced to undertake this work once again. The ticket collector without any passengers does not look particularly happy. However, if you look into his cabin a smiling visitor's face can just be seen.

Ticket barrier 4. New Brighton station, summer 1978. Class 503 unit No. 28690M waits to depart for Liverpool Central. New Brighton was once a popular Merseyside holiday/day-trip destination, but the 1970s witnessed its decline. This forlorn ticket barrier would once have been very busy.

Tickets please – Birkenhead Park, summer 1979. Since the earliest days of passenger railways ticket collection ensured passengers had paid for their journey – 'revenue protection' in today's language. During the 1970s the programme of station cost-cutting included the phasing out of this practice. While it did cut manpower costs, it made free travel an easy option for the less honest passenger. This narrow 1970s management thinking must have cost the North-West's railways more in lost income than they saved in manpower. Today's train-operating companies have recognised this loophole and now take action to minimise the risk.

Time for a chat – Birkenhead Park, summer 1979. During the 1970s the local station and its staff were still a significant part of many North-West communities. Sadly the staffing cutbacks that came with that decade would make this a thing of the past. In this quiet Saturday afternoon view the stationmaster takes time out for a chat with a local passenger. The Class 503 units berthed in the sidings would next be used on the following Monday's rush-hour services to Liverpool.

Guide Bridge, August 1979. This once-important station on the old Great Central route to London Marylebone (via Woodhead) was at the time largely intact with an ample complement of staff. The elderly porter just beyond the comfortable old station bench would easily have remembered the halcyon steam days, probably having fifty years of service under his belt. He is seen holding important inter-station railway documents to be handed to the guard on the Stockport–Stalybridge service which was shortly to arrive. Class 506 unit No. M59607M is arriving with a train for Manchester Piccadilly.

Mail by rail 1 – Manchester Victoria, March 1974. Station staff seem a little reluctant to load the stack of well-filled mailbags on to the Leeds-bound Calder Valley Line DMU.

Mail by rail 2 – Skipton, Easter 1979. Empty mail trolleys line Platform 2. These ancient pieces of equipment would be fully utilised in the early morning and evening when incoming and outgoing trains would take charge of the town's longer-distance letters and parcels.

CHAPTER TWO

Loco-hauled

Today loco-hauled coaching stock trains are few and far between, with those that do run often commanding many column inches in the railway press.

During the 1970s the situation was very different. There were hundreds of workings, including Inter-City, secondary passenger/summer Saturday trains, vans (mail/parcels/newspapers) and Specials (excursions/football trains) – throughout the North-West, all of which generated a great deal of locomotive and stock variety.

Unfortunately the commercial, economic and social changes that took hold during the 1970s would ultimately consign this very interesting part of the North-West rail scene to history.

INTER-CITY

The North-West's Inter-City services were based on the West Coast Main Line (north–south) and TransPennine (east–west) axis. This highly successful 1960s concept transformed the movement of passengers from/to major towns and cities by train. By the 1970s Inter-City had become a household name; its bright modern image was a hit with the travelling public and helped to stem the flow of passengers being lost to other forms of transport, especially the motorcar.

Wherever possible, Mk II (all variants) and later in the 1970s Mk III blue and grey liveried stock, complete with Inter-City branding, was used. This stock was supplemented by later-build Mk I coaches, either as complete rakes or augmenting trains particularly with full brake and catering vehicles.

As Inter-City's target market included the high income-generating business passenger, the Manchester and Liverpool Pullmans were a feature of the first half of the 1970s. The specially constructed and liveried Mark II Pullman car sets were well appointed and led a cosseted (out and back once a day, weekdays only) existence. Operational economics and the increasing popularity of business air travel meant that these premium services were soon withdrawn and the luxury coaches were put into store at Willesden where they suffered badly at the hands of local vandals. Ten examples did survive, however, and now form the West Coast Railway Company's 'Lakeland Pullman'. During the latter part of the 1970s British Rail did for a short while venture into this sector of the market again with specially branded and named new Mk III stock.

The North-West's Inter-City trains using the West Coast Main Line served London Euston, Birmingham, Cardiff, Plymouth, Southampton and Scotland. The Liverpool/Manchester to Glasgow/Edinburgh service was unusual in that it split/joined at Preston and Carstairs, often resulting in passengers not ending up where they were expecting to be.

Sleeping car travel was a notable 1970s West Coast Main Line Inter-City anomaly – a throwback to the days when it took many hours to get to and from London. Despite dramatically speeded-up services, Barrow-in-Furness, Carlisle, Holyhead, Liverpool, Manchester and Preston had the luxury of sleeping car services to and from the capital complete with crisp white bed linen, smartly attired stewards and morning tea and biscuits. As the sleeping cars often arrived at their destination many hours before breakfast time, it was common practice for them to be detached from the main train, enabling passengers to continue their sleep rather than being asked to vacate their cabins in the early hours. By the end of the 1970s it was clear that the sleepers' necessity and popularity was waning and today only the Anglo-Scottish services remain.

Until 1974 Inter-City West Coast Main Line services north of Crewe were in the capable hands of double-headed Class 50s. This combination in full flight on a heavy train was quite something

Carlisle, May 1975. An as yet unnamed Class 87 arrives with a Glasgow Central to London Euston Inter-City working. At the time the locomotive and Mk II air-conditioned passenger stock were 'state of the art'. The Mk I full brake was provided for post and parcels and was a common feature until the introduction of DVT push-pull operation during the 1980s.

to behold and literally an earth-moving experience. That year brought the full electrification of the West Coast Main Line, which required extra AC electric motive power. To satisfy this need the mothballed Class 82/83/84 locos were liberated from storage depots such as Bury and refurbished. These locos had not been well-received when first supplied by their English Electric, Beyer Peacock and North British builders and this stigma remained with them after their second incarnation, often playing second fiddle to their Class 81/85/86 brethren. This situation became even more apparent with the full introduction of the highly capable Class 87; by the time the 1970s were coming to a close Class 82/83/84s were no longer rostered for Inter-City work.

East–west Inter-City trains were the preserve of Class 40, 45/46 and 47 haulage, and during the late 1970s the occasional Class 55 'Deltic' which plied the Liverpool Lime Street via Chat Moss to Manchester Victoria then to Yorkshire through Standedge Tunnel axis. This popular service was until the later part of the 1970s augmented with Swindon TransPennine DMUs serving Hull, the rerouting of this service to Manchester Piccadilly bringing extra loco haulage (mainly Class 40s) via Victoria to York.

Adding to the loco-hauled Inter-City variety were the Midland interlopers, the 'Thames–Clyde Express' (Carlisle to London via the then threatened Settle and Carlisle Line) and the Manchester

Piccadilly to London St Pancras (via Hope Valley) trains – a throwback to the London services that served Manchester Central prior to its closure. Also, the Eastern Region operated the 'Harwich Boat Train' which ran between Manchester Piccadilly and Harwich, connecting with the Sealink Hook of Holland ferries. This train's circuitous route served many cities on its way to the east coast seaport. The train dated back to Great Central/LNER days when it originated at Liverpool, and even in the 1970s its provenance was clearly evident in the form of a teak-bodied Gresley buffet within the train's rake.

SECONDARY PASSENGER/SUMMER SATURDAY TRAINS

During the 1970s the amount of passenger traffic generated at rush hour on bank holidays and summer Saturdays was far too great for the normally rostered electric and diesel multiple units to cope with. This necessitated the 'big guns' being brought out in the form of loco-hauled rakes of Mk I stock either on relief workings or as high passenger capacity multiple unit replacements. These workings would be hauled by anything that was available and suitable, drawn from depots throughout the North-West. These workings often held many surprises and opportunities for rare haulage as the motive power possibilities included Classes 24, 25, 40, 45, 46, 50, 81, 82, 83, 84, 85, 86 and 87. Additionally, during the mid-70s when the Class 50s' work on the West Coast Main Line was at an end, the introduction of the Manchester Victoria to Barrow-in-Furness service made use of these fine locomotives. Unfortunately the Class 50s' transfer to the Western Region to replace the Class 52s soon brought this superpower haulage opportunity to an end.

A Class 85-hauled train seen at Moore (south of Warrington) racing towards Crewe with a West Country-bound Inter-City working, summer 1978. The fine steel girder bridge in the far distance takes the West Coast Main Line over the Manchester Ship Canal.

Summer Saturdays were not the only holiday season trains that required loco haulage; the long-distance, heavily laden Friday night trains to Paignton and Newquay also called on the services of a variety of motive power. As the 1970s marched on, passenger loadings began to wane as people started to be more reliant on the motorcar, especially as the motorways and improved A roads made it quicker to go by car than train. Low-cost air travel also began to nibble away at the holiday market; fewer people were heading to the traditional seaside resorts for their holidays. Eventually these factors combined to bring this aspect of loco haulage to an end. While very interesting for the enthusiast, this method of satisfying demand was costly, requiring run-round facilities, loco servicing, light engine and ECS (empty coaching stock) movements, together with yards filled with erratically utilised locos and coaching stock.

Today passengers are returning to rail travel, and the operating companies' answer to increased demand is frequent DMUs with high-capacity seating – economically far more sensible.

VANS

The term 'vans' is derived from the General Utility Vans (GUV) coaching stock often used on mail, parcels and newspaper trains; it could easily be confused with freight wagons such as Vanfits. During the 1970s Van trains were actually made up of a motley mix of LMS, SR, LNER and BR full brakes, GUVs and occasionally passenger stock. Their workloads were plentiful at the time and it would have been impossible to imagine that one day the work would no longer exist.

Mail: During the 1970s rail was the prime mover for Royal Mail letters, a practice that went back to the earliest days of Britain's railways. The decade would witness the beginning of the end for one of British Rail's most important business sectors. Airfreight and road haulage had started to offer viable alternatives that within thirty years would make mail by rail history – unimaginable in the 1970s.

In the 1970s North-West letters were moved by rail in three ways. The first was via the crack Travelling Post Office (TPO) trains, the 'West Coast Mail' and 'Irish Mail' along with workings to Aberystwyth, the West Country and York being notable examples. While this novel method of sorting mail as the train sped to its destination lasted into the twenty-first century, one of the first withdrawals was during the 1970s – the 'Irish Mail'.

Non-TPO mail trains serving major North-West stations were however far more common. A section of station was generally laid aside for mail trains, and Bolton, Carlisle, Crewe, Liverpool and Warrington were typical hubs. Unlike in later years there were few rail-connected mail distribution centres in the whole of the UK; Manchester's Mayfield was perhaps the only true example in the North-West at the time. At smaller towns, Barrow-in-Furness, Rochdale and Stockport for example, a GUV or full brake (or two) would be left in a bay platform for unloading/loading with mail. A passing train (mail or passenger) would drop off and collect the mail during the course of the day.

Probably the most visible method of getting letters to destinations was in the brake section of passenger trains, such as Inter-City and secondary. This was a quick and convenient method piggybacking on existing direct services. This practice, however, often required vans to be added to the train's stock to accommodate the large numbers of mailbags involved. This occasionally applied to DMUs as well as loco-hauled trains.

As the 1970s unfolded the attractiveness of the new alternatives became apparent. The volume of mail being moved by train began to reduce noticeably, and one of the first casualties of this fall-off in volume were the pre-nationalisation vans, which by the end of the 1970s has become rare indeed.

Parcels: During the 1970s there were Royal Mail Parcels and British Rail's own Express Parcels service making use of many of the same facilities as letter post.

British Rail's own service offered a choice of 'door to door' using its distinctive-liveried delivery vans or a 'to be called for' service. In the case of the latter there were parcels offices at major railway stations where items could be dropped off and collected. During the 1980s the British Rail service was marketed as Red Star and Night Star, a premium-rate service which became popular for its express transit times. This concept was later exploited by road-haulage carriers, ultimately leading to the demise of the rail-borne service.

Newspapers: Many northern editions of daily newspapers were printed in central Manchester at either Deansgate or Withy Grove. They were produced in vast numbers during the late evening for distribution throughout the north of England during the early hours. A major part of the logistical jigsaw puzzle was the newspaper train. Manchester Victoria was the hub for this stage in the operation, its proximity to the printing presses and central position within the railway network making it ideal. Trains would typically be of twelve or more vans, which gives an indication of the vast quantities of newspapers to be moved. The stock involved tended to be specific for this work and was branded 'Newspapers'. Red Bank, now part of an apartment development, was its base. Incoming ECS would arrive there during the morning and leave for its next load during the late evening, a sequence of operation that had been perfected over many years.

Unfortunately the 1970s was also to be the last full decade for this long-established part of the North-West rail scene. New technology would lead to the transfer of newspaper production away from the city centre, making Manchester Victoria no longer convenient. In addition quick motorway transit times ultimately made the rail-borne part of the distribution chain unnecessary.

SPECIALS

An ideal way to make better use of excess coaching stock capacity, especially during the slack off-season months, and utilise idle freight locomotives at the weekend was the operation of Specials – excursions and football trains (Footex). They added extra variety and many surprises to the 1970s loco-hauled North-West rail scene, ensuring there was year-round interest for the enthusiast.

Excursions: Enthusiast charters represented a small fraction of British Rail's excursion market during the 1970s. Most business was actually generated by British Rail's own Merrymaker trains; each of its Regions operated these often epic, budget-priced excursions. These trains were very popular with the general public, typically requiring twelve Mk Is to satisfy demand. They were devised on the pretext that they provided people with a taste of the destination with a view to encouraging them to revisit for their holidays using full-price tickets. More often than not, however, they simply provided people with a very cheap trip out to places normally too far away to contemplate for a day trip.

Manchester's Rail House ran its own version of the Merrymaker – 'Explore Britain By Train – Special Trips at Special Prices' – which provided a mind-boggling array of cut-price travel opportunities. For example, on 4 March 1978 it ran the following trains: 1. Bournemouth, pick-ups including New Mills, Romiley, Hyde Central; 2. Gourock/Dunoon, pick ups including Stalybridge, Bolton, Preston, Lancaster; 3. Eastbourne, pick-ups including Atherton, Moorside, Pendleton, Stockport – all at £4 return! For the enthusiast these trains provided a superb way of exploring the nation's rail network, traversing routes that rarely saw loco-hauled passenger trains, and often being hauled by unusual motive power – double-heading and loco changes along the way were commonplace.

Incoming Merrymakers from around the UK regularly ran to popular North-West destinations such as Blackpool, Carlisle, Chester, the Lakes, Morecambe and North Wales, which brought 'foreign' motive power from the Eastern, Scottish and Western and occasionally even the Southern regions. They were just what the doctor ordered for platform-end spotters and certainly added to the enjoyment of the 1970s rail scene.

During the 1970s British Rail also continued to promote its long-established charter trains aimed at associations, social clubs and special-interest groups. Like Merrymakers, these trains also invariably had unusual starting points or destinations, which ensured even more loco-hauled curiosities. Sadly the coaching stock and locomotive cull of the late '70s/early '80s would make the cut-price excursion yet another thing of the past – great while they lasted though!

Football Trains (*Footex*): These Specials had long been a feature of the North-West rail scene as they moved vast numbers of supporters to away matches throughout the season. Before the creation of the motorway system high-capacity loco-hauled trains were the only effective way of getting fans to a fixture in time for kick-off. Until the late 1960s football supporters had been a well-behaved if high-spirited group of rail travellers, after which time hooliganism began to raise its ugly head. By the 1970s the movement of supporters by rail had begun to be a highly questionable part of British Rail's passenger train business. Wrecked carriage interiors, and menacing, unruly and violent behaviour fuelled by drink became commonplace and was at a level unimaginable today. Stations and trains required large numbers of police to quell the ever-present threat of trouble. By the late 1970s Footex trains no longer made commercial sense to British Rail and they began to be withdrawn. This initiative coincided with the motorway coach beginning to be favoured by genuine supporters and had little effect on football club turnstile figures. Unfortunately it was another element of loco-hauled activity that would be lost in the 1970s.

An unidentified Class 47 powers the 10.45 Glasgow Central to Nottingham train through the then closed Dent station, late April 1977.

With this photograph it doesn't take much imagination to think you are leaning out of the carriage droplight and taking in the bleak moorland air (and Class 45 diesel fumes). This is the 09.50 Glasgow Central to London St Pancras 'Thames Clyde Express' speeding along the Settle–Carlisle route, March 1974.

A Class 85-hauled Glasgow Central to Birmingham New Street Inter-City train enters Preston, May 1978.

Warrington Bank Quay, summer 1979. No. 87032 *Kenilworth* glides through with a Glasgow Central–London Euston train. Mk III stock had by this time become a regular feature on these trains, replacing early Mk II vehicles, but despite this a Mk I restaurant/kitchen car and full brake are included in the formation owing to the non-availability of more up-to-date versions of these types of coaching stock.

A Liverpool Lime Street to Newcastle Inter-City train heads across Chat Moss powered by an unidentified Class 47, August 1979. The new T registration moped proudly parked alongside the platelayer's hut was owned by a railway worker whose L-plate indicates that he had not yet secured a full motorcycle driving licence, which would have allowed him to purchase a more powerful machine.

That open door is very inviting if only you could climb into the photograph! This unidentified Class 47 has been entrusted with the job of hauling the 10.10 train to Newcastle. Liverpool Lime Street, April 1977.

The 13.21 to Plymouth prepares to depart from Liverpool Lime Street, April 1977. The Class 47 will take the train through to Birmingham New Street where another member of the class will be attached to the opposite end of the train.

No. 47488 arrives at Prestatyn with the 18.44 for Holyhead (ex-London Euston), 29 May 1977. The rail blue 'British Rail' enamel sign is prominently sited overlooking the station car park. It is unusual because it is not the regulation black-on-white version that replaced the Midland Region maroon signs.

No. 25104 powers east out of Manchester Victoria with a short train of 'Express Parcels' vans, 26 May 1977. The driver is making a run at the steep Miles Platting bank which will shortly confront the train.

A Class 40 heads for the Saddleworth moors with a Liverpool Lime Street to York train at Stalybridge, July 1978. Amazingly this location is virtually unchanged apart from the loco-hauled train and the billboards, despite the passing of almost thirty years. It is still possible occasionally to come across Fiat, Mini, Morris 1000, Vauxhall and Volvo cars like those in the photograph in the station car park.

An unidentified Class 47 passes
Conway Castle with a London
Euston to Holyhead Inter-City
working, June 1976. The old
goods yard is filled with
interesting classics – a Mk 10
Jaguar, a Rover P4, a Hillman
Minx, a late-model Ford Zephyr,
caravan and a Commer Tipper –
all of which have probably long
since been scrapped.

No. 86259 heads off into the
dismal Stoke-on-Trent weather
with a Birmingham New Street to
Manchester Piccadilly Inter-City
train, November 1978.

The Sunday afternoon Manchester Piccadilly to London St Pancras hauled by No. 45021 (note the 00 21 headcode) gathers speed as it passes through Reddish North station on a wet day during summer 1974. The little girl waving at the passing train on the Manchester direction platform will be approaching forty years old by now. Her dad is keeping a watchful eye on both her and the train – I wonder if they remember that day all those years ago.

The southbound 17.00 'Manchester Pullman' hauled by E3137 enters Stockport station, June 1973. This immaculately kept but short-lived train replaced the 'Midland Pullman' upon the full electrification of the Manchester to London route. Thankfully a rake of these superb Mk II-variant coaches still exists as the West Coast's 'Lakeland Pullman'.

A failed Class 45 at the head of the delayed Harwich Boat Train is brought into Manchester Piccadilly by a Class 40, summer 1979. The Mk I stock in the foreground forms a Cardiff train and the DMU in the background is bound for Buxton.

Sunday morning 'Drag' working, Manchester Piccadilly, April 1979. The driver of the Class 40 climbs down from his locomotive after coupling up to the Class 86-hauled Inter-City working to London Euston. A passenger can be seen loading his motorbike into the full brake, the leading coach. Today this would be an unlikely occurrence, Pendolinos not having heavy duty, high-capacity guards' compartments and motorcyclists generally preferring to use high-speed roads to get from A to B.

Steam heat. By the time this photograph was taken – April 1979 – steam heating on Inter-City trains was becoming rare: this is
the Harwich Boat Train at Manchester Piccadilly. The Ilford HP5 film that produced this photograph was only processed in 2004
– twenty-five years later! – demonstrating the remarkable long-term storage properties of this product.

A Class 47 makes its way through Salford at the head of the 16.35 Manchester to Edinburgh Inter-City working, 9 July 1977. In the far distance, above the road bridge, can be seen the then modern Granada TV offices and studios. The skyline surrounding it is now filled with a new generation of modern buildings put up to serve Manchester's vibrant business community.

This Class 47-hauled train is providing a bank holiday Monday relief service to Blackpool North, May 1979. The popularity of day trips by train to the resort was still high at the time and relief trains were a regular feature.

Preston, August 1979. Crewe-allocated 25051 gets its Manchester Victoria-bound relief working from Blackpool North under way.

Liverpool Lime Street, July 1979. A Class 25 has just brought in an empty coaching stock train from Edge Hill, while the Class 40 alongside has just arrived with a train from York.

An unidentified Class 47 creates plenty of 'clag' as its driver brings on the power after negotiating the tight curve through Earlstown station, summer 1976. The train originated at Holyhead and would terminate at Manchester Victoria in the late afternoon.

No. 40084 arrives at Chester with a Holyhead-bound train from London Euston on a typically wet day during the summer of 1977. The loco was substituting for the usual Class 47 that took over from AC electric power at Crewe. The distinctive semaphores were on borrowed time and would soon be replaced by colour light signalling.

Wigan Springs branch-allocated 25140 has a weekend break from its usual freight duties at the head of a summer Saturday train from Manchester Victoria to Llandudno, seen at Moore, July 1979.

A Class 40-hauled Bangor to Manchester Victoria train passes the caravan site at Moore during the summer of 1978. This is a superb location for spotting and photography: the West Coast Main Line passes beneath the road bridge I was standing on.

Celebrity green 40106 (now preserved) makes its way past Llandudno Junction's since demolished signal-box and array of semaphores, en route to Manchester Red Bank Carriage Depot with empty coaching stock during summer 1976. The large number of loco-hauled workings often led to these stock positioning/balancing workings in order to redress availability problems. The water in the foreground is part of the Conway Estuary, which no longer exists. During the 1980s this section was drained and filled to enable the A55 Expressway to be built.

The 09.30 Saturday-only from Great Yarmouth is seen passing Brinnington (Stockport) council estate, 6 August 1976. The sun was not shining but the warm day would soon have dried the washing on the garden line to the right of the photograph.

No. 25125 prepares to depart from Stoke-on-Trent with a Saturday-only working from Llandudno to Derby, August 1976. The wide-open windows, empty pop bottles and hot-looking passengers in the front two compartments of M35127 show how unusually hot 1976 was. The weather was far hotter than we experience in today's global warming-dominated world – it also lasted for months. Today the pleasure of such an occurrence would be spoilt by the inevitable prophecies of impending doom.

No. 40107 waits in the early morning mist with an 'Explore Britain by Train' mystery (seaside destination) excursion, March 1978. The Class 86 on the adjacent platform is leaving with an Inter-City train bound for London Euston.

No. 24085 waits with a Bangor-bound train at Crewe during summer 1975. The open door of the Mk I carriage is hard to resist – you almost feel you could climb aboard.

Class 40 No. 328 passes Manchester Victoria's pilot, Class 24 No. 5026, with an ECS working bound for Red Bank, September 1973. The lattice overbridge was for the sole use of station staff who found it particularly useful for the movement of mail, parcels and luggage between platforms. The 'Coastal' buffet on Platform 12 alongside the Class 24 was especially popular as a refuge for spotters on cold days (of which there were many).

No. 47437 stands at Manchester Victoria's Platform 14 with a relief working to Blackpool North, August bank holiday 1979. Alongside on Platform 13 stands a three-car Class 104 'White Stripe' unit, strengthened by a Buxton-based member of the same class (drafted in for the weekend), also bound for Blackpool. The driver of the DMU can be seen taking a breather before heading for the coast.

No. 85037 greets a parcels train hauled by 25264 from Chester and the North Wales area as it approaches Crewe North Junction, 29 January 1977.

Class 83 No. 83012 prepares to leave Stockport Edgeley with a southbound parcels train, November 1973.

Manchester Victoria Platform 11 looking towards the disused platforms of Exchange station. It's late on a Saturday night in July 1979 and 40181 waits to head west with its 'hot off the press' load of *News of the Worlds*, *Sunday Mails*, *Mirrors* and *Times*. The operation had been perfected over many years and ensured that households got their newspapers without fail on time, day after day, week after week.

End of the day. A Class 40 prepares to take its empty stock to Red Bank after arriving with its evening train from Bangor, summer 1979.

CHAPTER THREE

Units

Just like today, units – diesel multiple (DMU) and electric multiple (EMU) – went about their work largely unnoticed during the 1970s, being taken for granted by enthusiasts and travelling public alike. They were even shunned by many spotters who preferred the plentiful diet of motive power. This suggests that units were a bland and uninteresting part of the North-West rail scene, but this was far from the case.

DIESEL MULTIPLE UNITS

The 1970s were the heyday of 'First Generation' units (those built as a result of BR's mid-1950s Modernisation Plan). Their pioneering years during the late 1950s and throughout the 1960s had seen them effectively replace inefficient steam haulage on the North-West's local/suburban trains, many secondary passenger workings and a miscellaneous array of other duties such as summer Saturday trains, occasional specials and even several mail/parcels workings. By the 1970s their operational sphere was well and truly established in the North-West, where an interesting cross-section of products from the array of manufacturers engaged by BR to build DMUs in the late 1950s/early 1960s could be found hard at work.

Local Passenger/Suburban: This operational role became the 'First Generation' DMUs' longest North-West stronghold, starting with the innovatory, but short-lived, M79XXX series Derby Lightweights of the mid-1950s and ending in 2003 with Class 101 units on Manchester Piccadilly to Marple/New Mills services.

During the 1970s the Metro Cammell unit (two and three car) was an integral part of local and outer suburban services. Chester depot in particular had a large contingent, which served Crewe, the North Wales Coast route and Wirral, plus Manchester trains running via both Warrington Bank Quay and Northwich. These services were supplemented by the pretty Class 103 Park Royal units, which were also based at Chester. Sadly this small class was one of the first to be withdrawn; its uniqueness was ultimately its downfall.

The Class 100, an early DMU product from the workshops of Gloucester RC&W, was one of the more distinctive-looking 'First Generation' units going about their business on the North-West's local lines during the 1970s. These units were exiles from Scotland and were shedded at Longsight for the Manchester–Marple/New Mills services, a route that has long been a refuge for passenger stock nearing the end of its days.

The Class 104 units in their two-car form could be found rattling along on local services radiating from Manchester to places such as Bolton, Greenfield, Rochdale, Stalybridge, Stockport and Wigan. Buxton's allocation of three-car examples of the class, complete with a distinctive white cab roof, spent virtually all of their lives plying the picturesque outer suburban route to Manchester Piccadilly. The only time they strayed away from their regular haunts was when they were occasionally pressed into service on summer Saturday or special train duties.

Class 105 Cravens units could also be found on Manchester services. However, they really made their presence known on Fylde and Lancashire locals, serving such places as Bolton, Blackburn, Burnley, Colne, Darwen, Ormskirk, Southport, St Annes and St Helens.

The ubiquitous Class 108 in both two- and four-aspect headcode versions appeared to be the nomads of the 1970s North-West local rail system. Allerton, Chester, Newton Heath and

Longsight depots all had allocations of this highly dependable BR Derby product, ensuring they were spread far and wide. They will always be remembered for their virtual monopoly on Cumbrian and Merseyside local services.

In most large conurbations around the UK – Glasgow, London, South Wales and the West Midlands, for example – 'Suburban' DMU derivatives with slam doors at every seating bay were extensively employed. This was not the case in the North-West, where there was only a small contingent of this type of DMU – the Allerton-based Class 115. These units, like the Buxton 104s, rarely strayed from their designated route – Liverpool Lime Street to Manchester Piccadilly via Warrington Central.

Perhaps the most well-appointed DMUs engaged on local services were the robustly built BR Swindon 'Cross Country' units – the Class 120s – which were mainly refugees from the Western Region. While these units were generally used on secondary passenger services, they could often be found on local services around the Crewe and Chester area. Their unmistakable two large square front cab windows set these units apart from the crowd.

Apart from the plating-over of redundant headcode panels and new liveries – PTE (white with a black waist stripe) and Inter-City (blue and grey) – little noticeably changed on the North-West DMU scene during the 1970s. However, the Class 101 and 108 refurbishment programme, which got under way in the later part of the decade, quietly set the scene for the 1980s. Those units not benefiting from a comprehensive makeover would be the first to succumb to the early 1980s influx of 'Second Generation' Class 142s and 150s which heralded the end of the 'First Generation' DMU era.

Secondary Passenger: Where loco-hauled formations were deemed unnecessary, DMUs took the strain on 1970s North-West secondary passenger services. These workings fell into two categories: cross-country stopping and express trains. Whichever the case, variety (including several examples of DMU exotica) was guaranteed.

Chester-based Class 108 and 101 units making up a six-car set are seen leaving Prestatyn with the 18.30 to Stoke-on-Trent on 29 May 1977. The bank holiday weekend's heavy passenger loadings necessitated this unusual formation.

The epic Cumbrian Coast services which stopped at every station between Preston/Lancaster and Carlisle was invariably assigned to Class 108 units, whose panoramic windows and observation car-style forward/rear vision was ideal for taking in the route's fantastic scenery. This DMU staple diet, however, would only be broken upon arrival at Carlisle, where Eastern Region Metro Cammell units working the service from Newcastle and Scottish Region examples on trains operating on the Glasgow via Dumfries line could be found.

Further south, the Morecambe to Bradford/Leeds service via Carnforth and Skipton yielded plenty of Eastern Region delights such as the Derby-built Class 114, Metro Cammell 101/102/111s and occasionally BRC&W Class 110 'Calder Valley' units.

The intensively operated Manchester Victoria to Blackpool run had its own dedicated fleet of Newton Heath-based 'White Stripe' Class 104 three-car units. The simple addition of a broad white stripe to the BR blue body side set these units apart from the rest. This was one of the earliest examples of individuality being allowed to infiltrate BR's strictly upheld corporate blue image associated with the first half of the 1970s. Two-car Class 104s would invariably work the much lighter-used Manchester Victoria to Southport via Wigan Wallgate service.

Long-distance North Wales Coast services engaged the same units that operated the local trains along the route – Class 101, 103 and 108s – but they travelled at much higher speeds and stopped at fewer stations. The break from this uniformity came at Chester, where Gloucester RC&W Class 128 'Cross Country' units could be found sharing services with Class 120s to Shrewsbury and beyond along the ex-GWR main line via Wrexham.

Crewe also yielded Western Region-bound delicacies working the Central Wales Line to Cardiff; these included the rare Pressed Steel Class 121 'Bubble Cars' which were included in formations to give extra power over the undulating route.

Class 120 units also featured on the meandering Crewe to Lincoln service, which called at Stoke before making its long but interesting journey across the East Midlands and on to the county town of Lincolnshire – a true cross-country route.

The trans-Pennine rail link via New Mills Central brought many DMU surprises on Hope Valley services, which often continued beyond Sheffield to Doncaster or Lincoln. This ensured that the eastern extremities of Manchester were treated to visits from Yorkshire-allocated Class 105, 114 and Metro Cammell units. In the later1970s this array was supplemented by the use of BR Swindon's finest DMU products – the stylish ex-Western Region Class 123 'Inter-City' and Class 124 'TransPennine' units – on a newly introduced Manchester Piccadilly to Hull service which used the route. These two classes were the ultimate in 'First Generation' design and interior décor, eclipsed only by the Metro Cammell 'Blue Pullman'. They had been built for express secondary services and offered quality open and compartment (first and second class) seating. The late 1970s were sadly their twilight years and this duty was to be their swan-song. Since the early 1960s the Liverpool Lime Street to Hull secondary passenger service had been the preserve of the Class 124s and provided a touch of glamour to a Merseyside dominated by BR Derby products. By the late 1970s the 'TransPennine' units' reign was at an end, being replaced by hourly loco-hauled trains to York/Newcastle, and hence the 'cascade' of these units to the new Hope Valley routed service.

Manchester Victoria's secondary passenger service to Leeds via Summit Tunnel – the 'Calder Valley' route – brought additional DMU variety to the North-West in the form of the dedicated Class 110 units based at Neville Hill; these were supplemented by a variety of Metro Cammell products.

The DMU concept was designed to bring to an end costly loco-hauled passenger trains, but amazingly during the 1980s the opposite occurred. Class 31 loco haulage took over the Hope Valley trans-Pennine services (extended to Liverpool Lime Street), Southern Region Class 33 haulage was entrusted to Central Wales trains (extended to Manchester Piccadilly) and Class 37 haulage became a regular feature on ex-DMU rosters along the North-Wales Coast route – during the 1970s these initiatives would have been unimaginable. This meant that the 1970s was the last decade when many examples of 'First Generation' DMUs were fully utilised in the ways they had been designed and built. From the late 1970s displaced DMUs, most notably the Class 123 and

124 units, began to be consigned to the breakers' yard. Sadly this was at a time before DMU preservation had got under way, which meant many gems were lost to the recycling industry.

Other Duties: DMUs could also be found on summer Saturday holiday trains supplementing loco-hauled formations. As most examples ran as two- or three-car units, it was common to see them coupled together to make up trains equivalent to eight or more coaches long. This made quite a sight when they were in full flight with their purposeful-looking vertical exhausts billowing fumes skywards. Trains to Scarborough/Filey Holiday Camp (Butlins) from Liverpool Lime Street, and North Wales trains from Stoke-on-Trent were typical services employing long trains of DMUs. The demise of the summer Saturday holiday train through lack of demand meant that this operational practice would also be lost to the social changes of the 1970s.

Special trains – Merrymakers, enthusiast and private charters – were not always a loco-hauled roster; shorter journeys or those less patronised were assigned to DMUs. This would add to the North-West's DMU variety during the 1970s. For example, units from the West Midlands could occasionally be seen at Chester, and Buxton's 104s were known to stray to seaside destinations such as Llandudno.

The single-car Gloucester RC&W Class 128 and Cravens Motor Parcels Vans were the icing on the cake with regard to DMU variety. These units could be seen either attached to passenger DMU formations or working independently, sometimes hauling vans. These units came into their own when consignments of mail/parcels did not warrant a loco-hauled train but were too large to be carried in the brake section of passenger trains. Their sphere of operation included the West Coast Main Line, Chester and Manchester. They were very effective – quick and economical – but unfortunately by the end of the 1970s their workload had been depleted by competition from road haulage. The Cravens units were withdrawn and the Class 128s were redeployed in the South.

ELECTRIC MULTIPLE UNITS

During the 1970s EMUs did not fare any better than their diesel-powered counterparts with regard to popularity and recognition – probably far worse when taking into account the few examples that made it into preservation. DC- and AC-powered units were well represented on the electrified lines of the North-West and together they created another rich layer in the area's 1970s rail scene make-up.

DC: This method of powering trains pre-dates AC EMUs by many years and was also typically used on tramway systems and overhead travelling cranes. A notable trait with this form of propulsion is the longevity of the electrical equipment, often resulting in the items it is powering being used for far longer than originally intended. This applied to the North-West's vintage suburban electrics operating in 1970s Manchester, Merseyside and the Wirral.

Manchester's most elderly examples were the pre-nationalisation Oxford Road–Altrincham units, which just made it into the 1970s. The trains were made up of slam door – complete with leather strap-operated droplights – suburban stock of the type that had disappeared from the national rail system a decade earlier. These units were a true time warp, and something that did not go unnoticed by local enthusiasts who ensured a number of trailer cars were saved for future generations. After the units' withdrawal this line was converted from 1500 volt overhead power supply to 25 kV AC, which enabled through running of suburban services from Alderley Edge and Wilmslow. This lasted until the conversion of the Altrincham to Deansgate section into part of the Metrolink tram system.

On the eastern side of Manchester could be found the Class 506 (also 1500 volt overhead supply) operated service to Glossop and Hadfield from Manchester Piccadilly, part of the Woodhead route. These units were built by Metro Cammell as an integral part of this complete electric railway – opened in the early 1950s – thought at the time to be the perfect example of how Britain's railways should be in the future. Unfortunately this bold initiative instigated by the LNER soon became outdated when in the late 1950s AC power was adopted by BR for all future electrification projects. Class 506, however, did linger on throughout the 1970s and into the early 1980s when the route was also converted to 25 kV AC power and Class 303 units were drafted in from Glasgow to operate the service. A complete Class 506 unit was saved for preservation, but unfortunately a lack of impetus led to it being scrapped; only a cab remains.

Manchester's only third-rail electric system, which dated back to Lancashire and Yorkshire Railway days, was home to the two-car Class 504s. These relatively new units had replaced their veteran predecessors in 1962 and were similar in appearance to the more angular-shaped AC Class 304. By the 1970s the Class 504s were very much part of the north Manchester railway scene and provided the area's inhabitants with a reliable, swift service between Manchester Victoria and Bury. These attributes were no doubt due to the skilful ministrations of Bury Depot's (now the East Lancashire Railway's workshops and steam running shed) maintenance team. During the 1970s several stored Class 504s lurked within the depot still sporting their original Brunswick Green livery, which notably contrasted with the all-over blue and later Inter-City colour schemes applied to their operational classmates. The class ultimately gave almost thirty years' service, lasting until the third-rail system was replaced by Metrolink trams. Fortunately a complete example has survived into the twenty-first century and it is safely ensconced at Bury.

On Merseyside the limited 1970s DMU variety was more than compensated for by the area's third-rail suburban electric network's venerable ex-LMS multiple units. The Merseyrail system was split into two – the Liverpool, Southport/Ormskirk (LSO) and Wirral lines.

The LSO had its own fleet of 1940/43-built Class 502 units, which replaced stock dating back to 1904. The class ran as three- or two-car units powered by four English Electric 235hp motors which were said to have been originally destined for Poland (a wartime frustrated order). These units were synonymous with the environs of Liverpool Exchange (closed April 1977) and days out to Formby and Southport. They lasted until September 1980, by which time they had finally succumbed to the influx of newly built Class 507 units. A complete unit (M28361M and M29896M) was subsequently secured by the National Railway Museum and for a time ran on the LSO system in LMS livery.

The Wirral lines were the preserve of the narrower and shorter-bodied Class 503s, whose earliest examples dated back to 1938. A second batch was ordered in 1956 to replace units lost in a 1941 air raid and also the last of the American-styled Edwardian Mersey Railway stock built for the mainly subterranean section of the system. It is interesting to note that for a long time the Class 503 units benefited from Birkenhead North Depot's ex-Mersey Railway tradition of using wax to 'dry clean' the bodywork, which was obviously far superior to the deleterious effects of the acid-based cleaner applied to Class 502s by staff at the old Meols Cop Depot. The Class 503s could be found on the New Brighton, Rock Ferry and West Kirby branches, which served low-level Liverpool Central, Lime Street and St James. They were also gainfully employed between 1977 and 1981 on the newly electrified Garston to Kirkby service. The Class 503s enjoyed a long life, remaining in service until March 1985, by which time they had all been replaced by Class 508 units drafted in from the Southern Region. Car numbers M28690M, M29289M and M28720M made it into preservation, but sadly like their Class 502 sisters lead a mothballed existence. It would be far more fitting to see them in their native habitat.

AC: The North-West's protracted AC electrification of its section of the West Coast Main Line started with the Manchester Piccadilly/Liverpool Lime Street to Crewe lines during the early 1960s. This brought with it the introduction of the first AC EMUs – the Class 304 – intended for use on local/suburban services and ultimately stopping trains to Stoke, Stafford, Wolverhampton and Birmingham New Street. By the 1970s the completion of the electrification programme allowed the units to fulfil their original purpose and also work stopping trains north to Preston. The Class 304s were based on the Mk I suburban coaching stock design with a consist of five coaches. During the 1970s the fifth vehicle was withdrawn; it had non-corridor/gangway compartments which had become a danger to passengers who could find themselves trapped on a moving train with an unsavoury fellow traveller. By the 1970s the world was becoming socially more hazardous and several unpleasant incidents had already occurred in this type of compartment. The Class 304 was an integral part of the North-West rail scene for over four decades, and it is a shame that a complete example was not saved for posterity.

During the 1970s the North-West's other key AC EMU player was the handsome Class 310. Built between 1965 and 1967, these Mk II coaching stock-based units epitomised 1970s style – just like flares, Jensen Interceptors and *The Good Life*. While they were allocated to London's Bletchley Depot, Class 310s were a familiar sight on fast secondary passenger services between Manchester Piccadilly/Liverpool Lime Street and the Midlands, and occasionally deputising or supplementing on Class 304 rosters. After the 1970s loco-hauled trains took over much of the Class 310s' North-West workload and they returned to their London and Midlands haunts. In later years they carved a niche for themselves on Eastern Region services out of London. Unfortunately mid-life refurbishment robbed the class of their 1970s individuality and they became clones of the later Class 312s – only photographs and memories remain.

Class 310 unit no. 086 waits to depart from Manchester Piccadilly with an evening train to Coventry, April 1976.

An Eastern Region refurbished Class 101 unit in bright, but very impractical, PTE black stripe on white livery leaves Skipton with a Leeds-bound train, November 1979. The steam era's infrastructure is clearly visible in the photograph over eleven years after BR steam came to an end. Unfortunately the Skipton to Leeds electrification work during the 1980s would sweep away many of this North-West/North-East outpost's vestiges of a bygone age.

LEEDS

Left: A Class 114 unit on a Bradford–Morecambe working and a Class 101 on West Yorkshire service mingle with the Midland Railway/LMS artefacts at Skipton station on a misty February day in 1979.

Below: A three-car Class 111 Metro Cammell unit which was built to work express and secondary passenger trains – hence the four-aspect headcode panel above the destination blind (by then redundant and plated over) – plus a couple of two-car units wait for passengers at Morecambe station (now part of a retail and leisure development) on Whit Monday 1979. This photograph shows how, when available, units would be used instead of high-capacity loco-hauled trains on days when passenger numbers were greater than normal. This train, destined for Bradford, would normally have been made up of a two- or three-car unit but because of the popularity of the Lancashire resort with bank holiday day-trippers significant strengthening of the usual formation was necessary.

Opposite: An Allerton-allocated Class 115 four-car Derby-built suburban unit arrives at Liverpool Lime Street with a working from Manchester Piccadilly via Warrington Central, March 1979. The Class 47 is waiting to depart with a Newcastle-bound Inter-City train. Suburban units were far more common in the London/Home Counties area and were generally only found in the North-West plying the ex-Cheshire Lines route between Manchester Piccadilly and Liverpool Lime Street.

The 12.15 Saturday-only from Filey Holiday Camp speeds through Newton le Willows heading for Liverpool Lime Street on 16 July 1978. The train is formed of three sets of ex-works two-car Class 101 units in West Yorkshire PTE livery plus a BR blue-liveried example in largely original condition.

A Bangor-bound Class 108 unit passes the vast Penmaenmawr stone quarry on a winter's day in 1978. The quarry is still in operation today and supplies ballast for the North-West's railways.

A Longsight-based Class 104 two-car unit runs into New Mills Central on evening working to Manchester Piccadilly via Belle Vue during July 1979. Until 1970 the service from Manchester had continued to Hayfield (approximately 5 miles east), after which the route was truncated on the pretext that it would avoid costly maintenance of New Mills Tunnel. This reasoning soon lost credibility when trains terminating at New Mills were subsequently held in the tunnel to allow Hope Valley trains to pass through the station.

There are plenty of passengers wishing to use the Lincoln service arriving at Stoke-on-Trent on a Sunday afternoon in May 1975. The three-car Class 120 unit was filled to capacity by the time it departed – demand had unexpectedly outstripped supply on this occasion.

By the late 1970s redundant Western region Class 123 Inter-City units had been drafted in to supplement the far more handsome Class 124 'TransPennine' units on the improved Manchester Piccadilly–Sheffield–Doncaster–Hull service. This 123 is seen thundering through Strines station with an eastbound train in October 1979.

New Mills Central was a busy Eastern region/London Midland 'border' station during the 1970s. In this scene from August 1977 an Eastern Class 105 has just arrived with a Hope Valley stopping train from Sheffield. The driver has already changed the destination blind to Doncaster and the guard will soon give him the all-clear to head east. The Class 100 unit provided the 'seamless' connection for passengers to Manchester Piccadilly via Belle Vue.

A Cravens unit prepares to depart from Guide Bridge's Platform 2 with a Rose Hill to Manchester Piccadilly service, July 1979.

Class 103 Park Royal two-
car DMU stands beneath
the vast slate mountain at
Blaenau Ffestiniog station
with the 16.45 service to
Llandudno, 30 May 1977.
This station has long since
closed, having been
replaced by the ex-GWR
facility which is more
conveniently situated in
the town centre. It is also
an interchange with the
popular Ffestiniog narrow
gauge railway. Note the
Crosville bus garage to the
left of the guard who is
carrying the train's tail
lamp.

A Class 100 unit arrives at Guide Bridge with a Stockport–Stalybridge Paytrain on a sunny August day in 1979. The passengers are waiting for the following electric train (Class 506) to Glossop and Hadfield.

A Class 104 two-car unit makes its way across Reddish Vale with a Stockport-bound Stalybridge shuttle train on a September evening in 1976. The wagons stored on the redundant two lines of the four-track formation were waiting to be scrapped at the nearby Standard Railway Wagon workshops adjacent to Reddish South station.

A Class 105 Cravens unit departs from the bay platforms at Manchester Victoria with an 'Oldham Loop' train to Rochdale, July 1979. The 'TransPennine' unit in the adjacent platform forms a stopping train to Leeds. By this date these one-time premier league DMUs were often found on more mundane duties such as these.

A 'TransPennine' unit headed by 51951 waits to depart from Manchester Piccadilly with a Hull-bound train, October 1979. The staff at the unit's home depot – Hull Botanic Gardens – had made good use of the redundant headcode panel, making it very easy for spotters to identify the unit.

Manchester Victoria, February 1976. A Liverpool Lime Street-bound 'TransPennine' unit waits to depart from Platform 11 (the longest platform in the world!).

Rush hour – Manchester Piccadilly, October 1978. A brace of LNER-inspired Class 506 units on evening services to/from the east Manchester suburbs and the Pennine towns of Glossop and Hadfield.

A Class 506 unit headed by
M559408M runs into Guide Bridge
with a late-evening train bound for
Glossop and Hadfield, June 1978.

Interior and route map, Class 506 unit,
Manchester Piccadilly, October 1978.

Above: End of the line – Hadfield, summer 1979. The driver of the Class 506 unit makes his way to the other end of his train before taking it back to Manchester Piccadilly.

Left: On a quiet Saturday afternoon the guard talks to the driver of a Bury-bound Class 504 unit before its departure from Manchester Victoria, summer 1978.

Right: A Class 504 unit headed by M77158 drifts past Crumpsall station's signal-box as it enters the north Manchester suburban station en route to Manchester Victoria, May 1978.

Class 504 unit M65447 is reflected in the compartment window of a Leeds-bound Class 124 'TransPennine' unit, Manchester Victoria, summer 1979.

A Class 504 unit passes over a wet Radcliffe street as it heads towards Bury, May 1978.

An Inter-City-style blue-and-grey-liveried Class 504 unit rumbles above the dark satanic mills of Radcliffe, October 1979. Today the once common chimneys that littered the Lowryesque northern landscape are few and far between, having been felled by the likes of Fred Dibnah, the mill engine houses and factories they served having long since closed.

A Class 503 prepares to depart from a snow-covered Rock Ferry station on a freezing cold January day in 1978. The signal-box has just given the driver the 'peg' and the doors are about to be closed, probably much to the relief of the hardy passengers aboard the train.

A Class 304 unit formed of set no. 022 rolls into Stoke-on-Trent with a Manchester Piccadilly to Stafford stopping train, while no. 83011 prepares to depart from the adjacent platform with an Inter-City train bound for Manchester Piccadilly, winter 1979.

Class 304 four-car unit no. 027 draws into Stockport with a Birmingham New Street-bound stopping train during summer 1975. This service was particularly tedious when used instead of a missed/non-available Inter-City or secondary passenger service – it stopped at every station between Stockport and Birmingham, making it a very slow alternative.

CHAPTER FOUR

On Shed

The North-West's 1970s locomotive, unit and coaching stock totalled many thousands: where were they all stabled, maintained and repaired? Depots, stabling points and workshops at strategic points throughout the North-West provide the answer. These locations were packed with interest for the enthusiast and in many cases the facilities had changed little since the days of steam. The people who worked at these places were a special breed who by and large ensured that the North-West's passengers and freight were kept moving without a hitch – skills built up over many years ensured this. However, by the end of the 1970s modernisation and rationalisation meant that this was also the swan song decade for the North-West's depots and sheds.

DEPOTS

Depots, as now, provided the facilities where the motive power, DMUs/EMUs and coaching stock were maintained and repaired, one step down from workshops. The difference between the 1970s and today is that there were more of them, they were well filled and – most importantly to the enthusiast – they were generally easily accessible.

The North-West's 1970s allocation of Class 08, 24, 25, 40, 47 and 50 diesel locomotives were dispersed between Birkenhead, Carlisle Kingmoor, Crewe, Edge Hill, Holyhead, Longsight, Llandudno Junction and Springs Branch. Class 81 to 87 electric locomotives and Class 304 and 310 EMUs were based at either Crewe or Longsight. Bury MPD, now the East Lancashire Railway's workshops, was home to the Manchester–Bury Class 504 EMUs. Birkenhead North catered for the maintenance needs of the LMS-design Merseyrail Class 502 and 503 EMUs. The venerable LNER-inspired Class 76s and 506 EMUs were cared for at Reddish whose extensive facilities attracted major diesel locomotive plus Bury, Merseyrail and AC EMU repairs.

The modern cleanliness of these depots was in stark contrast to many of the diesel facilities, which were generally converted steam sheds – very atmospheric but not the best environment for maintaining electric motors, hydraulics and switchgear.

The North-West rail scene featured a large array of 'First Generation' diesel multiple units – BRCW 104s, Cravens 105 and single-car parcel units, Derby lightweights/suburban, Gloucester 100/128, Metro Cammell variants, Park Royal, Swindon Inter-City 120 units – allocated to depots specialising in their maintenance. Allerton catered for Merseyside's fleet, Buxton looked after the Manchester–Buxton line's 104 units (easily identified by a white cab roof), Chester was in charge of units serving Welsh and Wirral routes, Longsight catered for south and east Manchester operations and Newton Heath took care of the units that served Cumbria and Lancashire (including the 'White Stripe' Manchester–Blackpool trains). To add to this variety, these depots also regularly provided their services to locomotives (especially at weekends) and occasionally attended to inter-regional visitors such as the Western Region's Pressed Steel units plus Swindon 'Inter-City' and 'TransPennine' units.

The 1970s were certainly the decade of the 'First Generation' DMU. However, the early 1980s and the appearance of the first 'Second Generation' units – the 150s – meant their days were numbered. Modernisation and standardisation would slowly eat away at the North-West's wonderful DMU variety, which would lead to reduced depot workloads and ultimately the closure of Buxton.

The vast amount of coaching stock needed for the North-West's cross-country, football, Inter-City, mail, Merrymaker, newspaper and summer Saturday trains also required maintenance, repair and storage facilities. Carlisle, Crewe South, Edge Hill, Llandudno Junction, Longsight, Red Bank (Manchester) and Stockport Edgeley provided the answer. The cost of operating such a large fleet of coaching stock, which was rarely fully utilised, was immense. Depot yards could often be seen full of BR Mk Is (all variants) and pre-nationalisation full brakes/GUVs awaiting the call of duty. By the end of the 1970s this system that dated back decades was beginning to come to an end. Service rationalisation would lead to thousands of coaches going to the breaker's yard and ultimately the closure of virtually all the depots.

STABLING POINTS

While not having the comprehensive facilities of a depot, stabling points provided basic maintenance and often refuelling facilities. They were generally located close to major junctions or rail hubs. During the 1970s the North-West's tally included Barrow-in-Furness, Blackpool, Carlisle Upperby, Ellesmere Port, Guide Bridge, Llandudno Junction, Northwich, Preston, Warrington and Workington. These locations could provide hours of enjoyment for the enthusiast because of the frequent comings and goings of locomotives and units. At weekends these stabling points became storage yards and provided great places for spotters to fill their notepads, especially as 'foreign' locomotives could be found lurking within the line-ups. It was not unusual to find Western 47 namers together with Eastern and Scottish Region delights – the unsolved puzzle was how did they get there in the first place?

WORKSHOPS

Crewe and Horwich were impenetrable (for the casual enthusiast visitor) and therefore were the ultimate 1970s North-West on-shed experience. Within these vast facilities, whose history dated back to the early days of the North-West railway system, heavy engineering at its very best prevailed. Locomotive construction and/or complete refurbishment was their forte. Notably Crewe manufactured the highly successful Class 87 electric locomotive and HST power cars during the 1970s.

Like the many other large general engineering complexes which were still a common feature of the North-West at the time, they also provided ancillary departments such as administration, building maintenance, electrical, painting, pattern making, foundry, machining and steel fabrication employing large numbers of people, many of whom worked there all their lives.

Open days or society works tours were generally the best way of gaining access to these marvellous places. Within their high walls and security fences could be found 'cops' galore. For example, at Crewe Works Scottish Class 26s and 27s could be found receiving attention.

The changing face of the North-West rail scene, which began in the 1970s, would ultimately bring the closure of Horwich Works and the preparation of Crewe for privatisation.

Winter reflection – Birkenhead MPD, January 1978. No. 25285 and two of its classmates share the depot's yard during the weekend lull in Wirral freight movements. The previous evening's snowfall has begun to thaw, creating puddles and slush that would soon freeze as the day quickly turned to night, making the yard particularly treacherous.

End of shift – Birkenhead MPD, January 1978. The young fitter is obviously a good listener, despite the harsh weather conditions. The pair had been undertaking weekend maintenance on the two Class 40s and would have welcomed the relative shelter of the ex-steam depot's main building, despite it being shorn of most of its roof!

Two stored 502 units share Birkenhead North Depot's yard with a brake van, used as part of the consist during their journey across the Mersey, August 1979. These vintage units would soon receive the call of the scrap man. Most of Merseyrail's 502 – and five or so years later the 503 – units would be cut up at either Birkenhead Depot (Mollington Street) or Cavendish Sidings.

Western Region 47080 *Titan* and a 108 unit share Liverpool Edge Hill Depot, winter 1976.

On a quiet Saturday morning in winter 1979 a Class 47-hauled Footex heads out of Liverpool past Edge Hill carriage sidings filled with Mk Is. During the 1970s there were thousands of Mk I coaches in capital stock for use on anything from Inter-City to local relief trains. While this allowed a great deal of operational flexibility, in reality few coaches were fully employed and by the end of the 1970s the decision had been made by British Rail to cut back on this far from cost-effective operational approach. This decision was also triggered by the ongoing reduction in Footex, Merrymaker and summer Saturday trains which had taken up a degree of surplus stock capacity. Eventually scores of coaches would be despatched to the breaker's yard. Thankfully a small proportion made it into preservation and still fulfil a vital role carrying passengers on Britain's thriving steam railways. In the distance (to the right of the photograph) is Liverpool's Anglican cathedral.

Llandudno junction carriage shed, Easter 1976. No. 40022 and an ex-works condition member of the class await their next turn of duty.

Class 40 no. 250 (40050), standing alongside Class 47 no. 1787 (47306), waits its next turn of duty after making a delivery of stores wagons to Newton Heath Depot, 17 November 1973. This depot was a regular haunt for spotters, being a short train journey from Manchester Victoria to the adjacent Dean Lane station. Today the depot is like Fort Knox; the casual visits of old are impossible.

In a scene reminiscent of the 'Big Four' pre-nationalisation publicity photos of their Top Link locomotives this photograph shows LMR's equivalent for winter 1974: 86204, 86042, 83011 and an unidentified 86/0.

No. 47446 stands within the ex-steam shed environment typical of the 1970s: Longsight, New Year's Day 1978.

Another Longsight Depot shot from New Year's Day 1978. Here a Class 25, 47 and 108 can be seen sharing the confines of the old steam shed.

Longsight carriage shed, summer 1977. A brace of immaculately presented Class 304 units (006 and 003) bask in the afternoon sun before their rush duties on Altrincham, Alderley Edge and Wilmslow (via Styal) suburban services.

Time for a fag – Reddish Depot, June 1979. The first signs of the new world of Health and Safety at work can clearly be seen on the Stothert and Pitt travelling crane. While the depot is clean in comparison with many of its contemporaries, there are one or two trip hazards that have gone unnoticed.

Mk Is at Longsight Carriage Depot, June 1978.

Horsepower. Three young horse-riders skirt Reddish Depot, August 1978. Today this pathway is so overgrown it is impassable and the depot has long since been reduced to rubble.

The shed cat stands at the window of Reddish Depot's foreman's office.

Empress of Canada (40032) undergoes heavy repairs at Reddish Depot, summer 1978. This well-equipped depot enabled it to become a virtual annexe to Crewe Works, the major work that can be clearly seen in the photograph being a regular occurrence.

A Class 40 stands outside Reddish Depot, August 1979.

No. 40035 A*papa* undergoes nose-end work at Reddish Depot, summer 1978.

The Midnight train to Georgia. The body side of withdrawn 24005 (D5000) has received the attentions of someone with a sense of humour. Was he called Arthur? Reddish, October 1976.

Bury Electric Depot yard, summer 1979. All th ose years ago it was unimaginable that today this overgrown expanse would be filled with operational steam locos and rolling stock – it is now East Lancashire Railways' Steam Depot and Ian Riley's locomotive workshops.

Guide Bridge stabling point, July 1979. The two Class 76s await their next call of duty from nearby Dewsnap Sidings. These locos would take night freights across the Pennines via Woodhead to South Yorkshire.

Class 25 no. 7589, an unidentified Class 47 and 76003 are seen taking a weekend break at Guide Bridge stabling point, 12 January 1974.

No. 24082 and an unidentified ex-works Class 40 inside Llandudno Junction Carriage Shed, Easter 1976. After the ex-LMS steam shed was closed in the early 1970s 'the Junction' became a busy stabling point, seeing a great deal of activity owing to the large amount of 1970s North Wales loco-hauled passenger traffic, especially on summer Saturdays. By the end of the 1970s this type of traffic was beginning to come to an end and the buildings/yard found a use as DMU and EMU storage. Over the ensuing years the buildings became more and more dilapidated, and by the 1990s they had succumbed to the bulldozer. The land is now used for food/retail units, which are particularly popular because of their proximity to the Holyhead/Queensferry Expressway.

The unusual sight of a young family adjacent to the traverser where ex-works Class 25, 40 and 47s are proudly displayed. Crewe Works Open Day, 20 September 1975.

CHAPTER FIVE

Freight

Coal, engineering, manufacturing, steel, ports and shipping were very much part of the 1970s scene, especially in the industrial North-West. For generations these industries provided employment to thousands of people and underpinned the socio-economic fabric of the region.

Unfortunately, the effects of the 1970s' industrial unrest – electricity blackouts, the three-day week, 25 per cent inflation, company closures, large-scale unemployment – demonstrated in the worst possible way how prominent these industries were in the community as a whole.

The turmoil triggered commercial and political changes that would consign many industries to the history books or leave them shadows of their former selves.

During the 1970s much of industry – especially larger enterprises – still relied on rail for the movement of raw materials and finished goods. The demise of long-established customers and a growing motorway network, which would ensure the artic became the future's number-one freight-mover, meant that the 1970s was the last full decade of old-style rail freight.

Since the start of the Industrial Revolution the North-West had made full use of its rail system to develop and prosper, and over a 150-year period the region's railways were an integral part of the industrial economy. To serve the demand a huge array of facilities and methods of operation had become established over the years, and during the 1970s they remained largely intact.

Goods depots serving major towns and pick-up freights calling at rail-connected companies were still commonplace. Sidings and marshalling yards such as Dewsnap, Edge Hill and Workington were often close to residential areas, and that unmistakable sound of loose-shunted wagons was an accepted part of everyday life – day and night.

Air-braked block trains – aggregates, coal and Freightliners – were in the minority. Loose-coupled and vacuum-braked short-wheelbase wagons predominated, several of which dated back to pre-nationalisation days. Just a few years later they would be swept away in their thousands, yet at the time it would have been difficult to imagine a railway without the ubiquitous 16-ton mineral wagon and the friendly brake van, a necessary feature of virtually every train.

Large numbers of people were needed to make up the trains. Shunters and other yard staff worked in all weathers, which could be quite perilous. Many yards were sparsely lit, often relying on gas lamps, grime-encrusted electric light or oil hand lamps. This made working at night or in the industrial smogs (despite the 1964 Clean Air Act) particularly dangerous. The summer heat and winter ice and snow made the physically demanding work – bending, climbing, jumping, lifting, running, walking – even more challenging. During the 1970s this was accepted as 'what we've always done', but by the mid-1980s much of it was a thing of the past.

During the 1970s, just as in steam days, there was a large presence of freight and mixed-traffic locomotives throughout the North-West region. The large-scale reduction in freight activity would lead to the mass withdrawals of motive power. By the end of the decade the Class 24, 25, 40, 45, 46, 76, 82, 83 and 84 had either disappeared or were disappearing from their North-West haunts.

To get a feel for the extent of 1970s North-West freight activity, a brief resumé follows. How times have changed!

COAL

Coal and its derivatives emanating from NCB (National Coal Board) pits in Cumbria, Lancashire and North Wales (all now closed) were extensively burned by domestic and industrial users. Many thousands of tons a week were moved by rail, using long rakes of 16-ton short-wheelbase wagons or the larger capacity HAA ('Tubs'). As pits and distribution depots were often located away from the main line, there were numerous 'Freight Only' lines scattered around the North-West. These were invariably truncated remnants of the 1960s Dr Beeching cuts, which had closed many routes. These backwaters of the rail system received little maintenance. Trains often had to contend with ever-encroaching vegetation, fly-tippers and locals using the routes to take short cuts. At the end of these lines a hidden delight – steam – could often be found. Pits still used steam power, coal being readily available, and it could be seen in action hauling heavy trains of BR coal wagons to the exchange sidings.

Coal was important to everyone: it was relied on for electricity generation, which was clearly emphasised during the 1970s coal strikes. The CEGB (Central Electricity Generating Board) needed vast quantities to keep the region's numerous power stations running. So great was the demand that supplies had to be supplemented with trainloads shipped via the Woodhead route from South Yorkshire. Several power stations such as Agecroft and Heyrod also used steam engines to shunt 16-ton mineral wagons into tipplers, which fed the boiler room via a conveyor. Today's modern power stations are gas- or nuclear-powered, and only Fiddlers Ferry remains as a major coal-burner. The once-familiar yards filled with coal wagons beneath huge cooling towers are very much a thing of the past.

STEEL

Steel was also needed in vast quantities to satisfy the North-West's needs – far more than is used today. It was the base material for many of the region's key 1970s industries, such as armaments (Royal Ordnance and Vickers), building, civil engineering, cars (Ford, Triumph and Vauxhall), engineering (light to heavy), railways (BR Castleton, Crewe and Horwich) and shipbuilding (Cammell-Laird and Vickers). At the time the North-West could boast four major BSC (British Steel Corporation) plants – Irlam, Shelton, Shotton and Workington. Today only a scaled-down Shotton

Fiddlers Ferry, August 1979. An NCB Dodworth Colliery consignment label on an HAA wagon. Dodworth pit was in Barnsley. The coal was shipped via Penistone over the Woodhead route to the Merseyside power station. Today Dodworth Colliery has long gone and a modern industrial estate occupies the site.

and Workington remain. In addition, there were several independent producers, which included Bredbury Steel, Johnson & Nephew (specialising in wire) and Manchester Steel, all now closed. Much of the steel produced relied on British Rail for distribution and incoming raw materials such as iron ore. The tonnages generated were immense and the gradual rationalisation of the industry, starting with BSC Irlam in the early 1970s, was to be another significant loss to the North-West's rail freight customer base.

CHEMICALS

Chemicals were a North-West speciality: ICI (Imperial Chemical Industries) at Buxton, Fleetwood, Northwich, Runcorn and Widnes was the largest producer, and its raw materials and finished products were often to be seen plying the region's railway routes. ICI branded wagons were easily recognisable, especially the limestone trains which operated between the plants at Buxton and Northwich. These pre-war trains were the forerunner of today's block trains; the large-capacity vacuum-braked hopper bogie wagons were intensively used, their high availability rate being ensured through good maintenance at the company's Northwich Workshops.

Before the introduction of pipelines petrochemicals also featured highly on the 1970s North-West rail scene. Shell Stanlow in particular created much inward and outward traffic. Nearby Associated Octel provided the vital ingredients for creating two-, three-, four- and five-star petrol. This company had regular trains running to its other plant at the end of the freight-only branch line at Amlwch, Anglesey.

CONCRETE AND STONE

The continued buoyancy of the construction industry has ensured that much of this high-volume heavy traffic remains the preserve of rail freight. However, until the 1970s much of the work was entrusted to short-wheelbase wagons. The Presflo wagons operated by Blue Circle at Hope were a common sight throughout the North-West region, particularly with the popularity of pre-cast concrete during the 1970s.

IMPORTS AND EXPORTS

British Rail served all the North-West ports of Birkenhead, Ellesmere Port, Heysham, Holyhead, Liverpool, Manchester and Preston during the 1970s. Port closures, rationalisation and road haulage would combine to reduce rail-borne tonnages considerably by the 1980s. Only containerisation would ensure the railways kept a foothold in this sector of the market. However, even the Freightliner depots at Holyhead and Longsight would later close.

CARS

By the late 1970s virtually every family owned a car – ultimately having a negative effect on 1980s passenger travel. To get the vehicles to their customers in the quantities demanded, rail transport was ideal. Not only did Merseyside-built products make use of the North-West rail system, but so did the incoming British Leyland, Chrysler, Ford and Vauxhall models from the Midlands and south, as well as Hillman Imps from Linwood, Scotland. Today rail transportation is still used but the artic is by far the most popular means of getting the product to the agents.

To add to this high level of 1970s freight activity, there were other notables such as sand for Pilkington's Glass at St Helens, Cornish clay 'hoods' for the Stoke potteries, Cheshire salt, fabrics, electrical goods and food (fresh and processed). By the end of the 1970s much of this work was fast becoming a part of railway history.

The closure of freight depots, lines, sidings, yards and wagon workshops, and the resulting job losses, meant that the 1970s certainly marked the end of an era for North-West rail freight.

Hot work. No. 08820 *Guide Bridge* and shunting gang move rail freight wagons into Ashbury's freight depot ready for loading with Johnson & Nephew wire coils, August 1979.

Jumping down. One of the shunting gang jumps down from the slowly moving 08 shunter while positioning a train of rail freight wagons loaded with wire coils, August 1979.

No. 25195 passes Crossley Engines (left) and a Great Central signal (right) with a mixed train of mainly loaded coal wagons at Ashbury's, April 1976.

A Class 25 passes beneath the footbridge on the approach to the closed Manchester Exchange in winter 1976. It is in charge of a short (two wagons and a brake van) train heading west.

Godley Junction, August 1979. A member of the yard gang attends to a train of well-loaded 16-ton coal wagons from the South Yorkshire mines.

Nos 76039 and 76036 leave Godley Junction with a loaded coal train bound for Ardwick, August 1979.

Having just brought a mixed freight into Dewsnap Yard, a Class 25 heads back to the Stockport area through Guide Bridge, winter 1978.

During winter 1974 a Class 08 heads towards Bredbury Sidings adjacent to Bredbury Steel, and is seen here crossing Woodley Junction. The line to the right is the route taken by Fiddlers Ferry coal trains through the closed Stockport Tiviot Dale station, then Broadheath and Lymm.

Petrochemical wagon – Guide Bridge, winter 1979.

No. 45044 brings on the power after crossing Romiley Junction with an ICI hopper train, July 1979.

It's 1.40 on a wet November afternoon in 1973. The driver of no. 318 (40118) has brought his long train of 16-tonners to a standstill on Manchester Victoria's through line and is attempting to communicate with the guard (just visible leaning out of the trailing van). The photograph's low viewpoint accentuates the steep incline out of Victoria, Miles Platting bank, which in steam days regularly made it necessary to employ a banking engine to keep heavy trains moving. This train is making its way back to the Lancashire coalfields for refilling after delivering coal to CEGB Chadderton power station. Note the trainspotter at the far end of Platform II. This location had been popular with enthusiasts for generations.

A Class 76 passes through Hadfield with a mixed freight at approximately 7.30 one evening in July 1979.

An unusual pairing of a Class 25 and Class 40 seen at Chester station having just arrived with a train of vans from Ellesmere Port in winter 1979. After the piloting 25 has been detached and run round towards Chester MPD the Class 40 will take its train to Warrington Arpley Yard. The scaffolded section at the end of the station canopy is the result of a freight train accident.

Pick-up freight – Llandudno Junction, August 1976. No. 25152's driver, shunting gang and brake van guard while away a few minutes together in the afternoon sun while awaiting further instructions. A few years earlier the train would have been much longer, but by this time it was clearly uneconomic and would not continue into the 1980s. Note the broken loading gauge on the left.

Llandudno Junction Yard, winter 1977. The driver of 40106 prepares to get his Amlwch-bound Associated Octel train underway. Note the yard gas lighting.

Mineral wagons fill the station yard at Stoke-on-Trent, winter 1978.

A Class 40 heads south through Wigan North Western with an empty car train, November 1972. The photograph was taken from Wigan Wallgate station. It was one of my first successful railway photographs, taken on a second-hand FED camera (£5 from Mr Dodd's photography shop, Gorton), a fourteenth birthday present (September 1972).

No. 40139 passes Kirkham with an ICI Fleetwood-bound train, August 1978. The line to the plant was the truncated route to the Fylde fishing port.

The driver makes his way to the signal telephone to enquire why he is being held at Carlisle Citadel station's signals in winter 1977. No. 47361 heads a North-West-bound LPG train. Note the barrier wagon because of the hazardous load.

Bickershaw Colliery, Lancashire,
2 March 1975. Hunslet 0–6–0ST
Austerity *Hurricane* pauses between
shunting HAA wagons.

Bickershaw Colliery, Lancashire, 2 March 1975. Hunslet 0–6–0ST Austerity *Hurricane* hauls a long train of 16 tonners to the BR exchange sidings.

CEGB Agecroft Power Station, winter 1977. RSH 0–4–0ST *Agecroft* 3 seen pausing between coal tippler shunting operations. Each train had to be pushed wagon by wagon through the tippler, which fed the power station boiler house via a conveyor that bridged the Manchester to Bolton line.

CEGB Agecroft Power Station, winter 1977. RSH 0–4–0ST *Agecroft* 3 is seen hauling empty 16-tonners to the BR exchange sidings. The winding wheel buildings of the adjacent NCB Agecroft can be clearly seen in the background.

Discarded lamp – Northwich, July 1979. No longer wanted, the lamp rusts away as nature takes over in the under-utilised goods yard.

Warrington, September 1979. A redundant goods yard building stands forlornly. Nature and vandals had already made their presence felt.

A withdrawn tank wagon moulders away in the Standard Railway Wagon Company's scrap line at Reddish South during the summer of 1974.

Lifted freight line – Denton, March 1974. An early victim of the 1970s reduction in freight. Most of this line's traffic was generated by the nearby 'Town Gas' NWGB (North Western Gas Board) plant. On conversion to North Sea gas the coal supplies were no longer required.

CHAPTER SIX

Safety First

Safety has always been a prerequisite of North-West railway operations since the earliest days of the Liverpool and Manchester Railway, but it was often dependent on custom and practice, proven methods along with robust – but antiquated – equipment. By the end of the 1970s this situation would no longer prevail, as a result of new stringent legislation, modern technology, the accountants' 'bottom line', and a developing blame and compensation culture – a powerful combination of influences that could not be ignored. Much of what had remained the same for decades would become a modern-day hazard, taboo or anachronism. A brief look at a few safety-related features of the 1970s North-West rail scene shows how these significant new forces ushered in the kind of railway system we have today.

PERMANENT WAY

Until the 1970s the installation, maintenance and repair of the permanent way had changed little in the North-West for a very long time. Many gangs could still be found using traditional equipment and methods which in some cases dated back to pre-Grouping days. The manual handling equipment and tools used would set alarm bells ringing in the ears of the modern safety official – Health and Safety Regulations were yet to be invented. Safety clothing had also changed little over the years. Caps and trilbies were only just beginning to be replaced by hard hats. Hi-vis jackets, a 1970s creation, were slow to become popular, let alone compulsory. Radio communication was also a new phenomenon: keeping a sharp look-out and a sixth sense were still heavily relied upon to keep danger at bay. Lineside facilities were also primitive: the precast-concrete platelayer's hut was the ultimate example of basic protection from the elements.

The permanent way itself was also undergoing a significant period of change during the 1970s. To the travelling public the most notable aspect would be the disappearance of the familiar and relaxing 'clickety clack' from most major routes as jointed track was gradually replaced with continuous welded rail. The transition, which continues to this day, gave a safer, smoother ride and enabled modern techniques to be adopted. The move away from the use of creosote (now deemed unsafe) soaked sleepers and heavy large cast-iron chairs (iron foundries are not the healthiest of places) to support the jointed rails was another safety benefit.

The rolling stock still used during the 1970s by the Civil Engineering (CE) Department to work on the permanent way was also still predominantly low-tech and largely a throwback to the steam age. Aged vacuum-braked flat, open and hopper wagons, and brake vans, were the principal means of moving materials. These items of rolling stock had curious names such as Dogfish, Sea Lion, Turbot and Walrus: how many enthusiasts have stood and wondered why these wagons had such unusual names? To provide accommodation for the track laying and lifting (a common occurrence in the 1970s) gangs, their trains often included an ex-passenger coach. By the 1970s these coaches were the oldest in use in the North-West. Examples of pre-nationalisation railway company products would remain in use until at least the end of the decade. Their late withdrawal gave preservation societies a second chance to secure examples of coaching stock that would have otherwise been lost to the 1960s scrap man – sadly, despite this only a few were saved. Only in the later part of the 1970s did modern technology begin to change the face of the CE Department's rail-borne equipment. Hi-tech ballast machines, tampers, track-laying equipment and ultra-sonic rail testing all came about as a result of a meeting of minds between the machinery manufacturers, the CE and the Research Department.

SIGNALLING

An all-important part of the 1970s rail scene was the signalling – an eclectic blend of many influences, from the earliest railway companies' through to the latest 'state-of-the-art' technology. This mix combined to ensure the safe passage of the many trains that used the North-West's rail routes during the 1970s.

The widespread use of vintage equipment resulted from a combination of reasons, including its effectiveness, longevity and reliability, plus necessity caused by minimal investment over previous years. At the beginning of the 1970s multi-aspect colour light signals were still in the minority. With the exception of Manchester Victoria with its 1929-vintage 'Clusters' and several electrified routes, much of the North-West rail system was still signalled by lower or upper quadrant semaphores (single pole, bracketed and gantry versions). These highly visible pieces of pre-Grouping/nationalisation and BR equipment abounded, helping to maintain a steam age image long after the last Black 5 was towed away to the breaker's yard. This situation was not to last; the resignalling of the West Coast Main Line north of Warrington, in preparation for the 1974 introduction of electric trains through to Glasgow, would be the precursor of things to come. This project not only streamlined the control of trains – hundreds of signal-boxes and thousands of

Men at work – Ashbury's, summer 1979. In the days before the Health and Safety at Work Act regulations, a six-man permanent way gang propels an ancient trolley (just look at those wheels) laden with sleepers and tools to site (opposite the old Beyer Peacock locomotive works), a task that had not changed since the dawn of the railway age. It is worth spending a few minutes to spot how many twenty-first-century health and safety breaches can be seen in this photograph.

semaphores were no longer required – it also did not go unnoticed by the travelling public. This highly visible fast forwarding into the modern world helped BR to regain passenger confidence and increase passenger numbers on its premier route, especially on Inter-City services. As the decade unfolded, the North Wales Coast and non-electrified TransPennine were notable additions to the rapidly expanding list of routes using multi-aspect colour light signals. Today there are just a few pockets of semaphore signalling – enjoy and photograph them while you can – notably in the Buxton area, and the Cumbrian Coast and Settle and Carlisle line, maintained by a dedicated, skilled team of specialists.

In many cases the signal-boxes were a lot older than the signals and track layouts they operated and controlled, a situation which in several cases prevails today. For example, Stockport station still retains its LNWR signal-boxes despite the comprehensive twenty-first-century modernisation of the electrified main lines south of Manchester Piccadilly. Like the semaphores, many signal-boxes would not survive the 1970s. Despite their imminent demise they remained the pride of the Signal and Telegraph (S&T) Department, and it showed. Their external condition was often immaculate, contrasting starkly with the decay and dereliction that typically surrounded them. Their interiors were a credit to the signalmen that worked them: polished floors, neatly tended coal stoves for cooking/heating, and gleaming levers and block instruments were the norm. During the 1970s the trainers of new signalmen continued to make use of the Lancashire and Yorkshire Railway's Bassett-Lowke model railway to simulate real-life situations. This superb artefact was housed within the upper floors of Manchester Victoria's grand offices (the headquarters of the Lancashire and Yorkshire Railway) until no longer required. It can now be viewed at the National Railway Museum in York.

An aspect of the 1970s North-West rail scene that would certainly make today's safety officer quake in his steel toe-capped boots was the telegraph pole. Mile after mile of them lined all major rail routes, supporting the wires for inter-railway communication. Imagine the risk levels associated with the lineman's daily task of scaling poles, often well over 20 feet high, in exposed locations such as isolated windswept moorland, to maintain, repair or replace insulators, timber and wire. The high level of risk was compounded by the minimal use of appropriate safety equipment. Today those thousands of miles of wire are safely buried alongside the track rather than strung high above it – an initiative that really got under way during the 1970s, making the high-wire skills and daring of the lineman redundant. I wonder how many people actually noticed the demise of the telegraph pole.

CROSSINGS

During the 1970s many road and bridleway crossings in the North-West had changed little since Victorian days, a time when traffic was much lighter and limited to one or two horse power. Wooden-gated crossings opened using a wheel in an adjacent signal-box or manually by a gatekeeper or the general public was still commonplace. These crossings were often lit by oil lamp and there was little warning of the imminent approach of a train. Their safety relied on good fortune, trust and efficiency of use. By the time the 1970s were coming to an end the realities of the modern world meant the potential hazards were becoming too high a risk for British Rail to tolerate.

Today many level crossings are permanently closed, having been replaced by congestion-beating bridges or modernised using half barriers complete with audio warning, electric lighting and CCTV surveillance – a far safer mix in an environment where the patient gentleman motorist is a thing of the past and road traffic is completely different from the days of the horse-drawn vehicle.

FENCES

Today hundreds, possibly thousands, of miles of severe but highly effective palisade fencing skirts the North-West's depots, routes and sidings. It is particularly in evidence in the inner cities and suburbs, having been deemed necessary to keep out crime, the foolhardy and the suicidal, as well as those elusive terrorists we are constantly reminded of.

During the 1970s we lived in a far more carefree, trusting world where people took responsibility for their own actions. There had never been a need to turn the railways into a fortress. Fencing did exist, but in a far less obtrusive and oppressive form. Over the decades it had sprung up in many different forms, often reflecting the materials and styles of the prevailing period: wrought iron and castings for the Victorian/Edwardian era, steel for the twentieth century, concrete panels from the 1930s. Strands of wire threaded through concrete uprights or more substantial chain-link fencing was particularly popular during the 1960s/1970s, being low-cost and easy to erect. From the dawn of railways wood, especially recycled railway sleepers – who said recycling was a modern concept? – also provided a barrier between railway property and public. This variety is still in evidence along North-West rail routes, but to a far lesser degree than in the 1970s.

The changeover to high-security fencing has made much of the North-West's lineside spotting locations no-go areas, which must surely have stifled many youngsters' interest in railways. Gone are the days when you could while away the hours watching trains go by perched on top of a sleeper fence or squeeze through a gap to reach a depot or yard filled with potential 'cops'.

SIGNS

Until the 1970s safety signs were relatively few and far between. There was a reliance on people to use their common sense to keep out of harm's way.

The majority of signs intended for the general public tended to instruct them not to trespass on the railway – the prospect of a fine was an effective deterrent. Being of a substantial nature (cast iron/enamelled steel), many of these signs had stood the test of time and dated back to pre-Grouping/nationalisation days. By the end of the 1970s the modern clinical signs we are now familiar with had all but replaced their predecessors. Those signs that were saved by collectors now command high prices at railwayana auctions. Today 'Do not trespass' has been supplemented with an array of signs designed to keep people safe and the prospect of compensation claims (almost unheard of in the 1970s) to a minimum.

Warning signs intended for the general public and railway workers alike were however in evidence along electrified routes and at level crossings. As electrification spread and crossings were modernised during the 1970s the number of these signs was increased and the less clear replaced with new unmistakable versions.

Safety signage, as with all industries in the 1970s, was also at a premium for the railway worker. Those that did exist were often 'home-made' – certainly not of the modern legislatively prescribed type used today – or railway company/BR London Midland Region standardised versions. These signs also added to the steam age feel of the railways during the 1970s, especially in and around loco depots.

On the lineside one of the most important signs was the profiled-steel speed restriction warning. These steam age signs were meant to have yellow painted numbers, but time in a dirty environment meant they became a dark grey/grimy yellow and were often quite difficult to see at night or on a dull day. Surprisingly a large number of these signs are still in use today, but now benefit from regular coats of yellow paint and a much cleaner atmosphere, making them far more effective. Eventually they will be replaced by the now common large highway-style reflective versions, but for now it is possible to see this modest, but vital, piece of railway heritage still in use along the increasingly modern lineside.

Block and tackle – Manchester Victoria, April 1978. From within the small CE workshop – probably unchanged since LMS days – a Class 504 unit can be seen departing for Bury.

In the days before regulation signposting home-made warning signs prevailed. In this instance Reddish Depot's resident comedian has deftly replaced a 'W' with a 'G', which certainly made people give this part of the depot a wide berth.

In stark contrast to the photograph on page 122, this one clearly shows that the modern world was making inroads into the North-West rail scene by the end of the 1970s. The CE Department's state-of-the-art DN 73266 is seen at around 10 p.m. on a July evening in 1979 before commencing work on the maze of trackwork within the environs of Manchester Exchange and Victoria. The chimney in the central background belongs to the original Boddington's Brewery and the tower/chimney to the far left keeps watch over Strangeways Prison.

Another example of the modern infiltrating the North-West rail system. BR Derby Research Department's Decapod 25 Laboratory Coach is seen heading north along the West Coast Main Line hauled by Springs Branch-allocated 25060 at Warrington Bank Quay, May 1978. It was not unusual during the 1970s to find these Research Department trains either hauled by one of their own oddities such as a Clayton or in the form of an early build Derby Lightweight unit.

No. 25104 hauls a CE Department spoil train, made up of a variety of vacuum-braked short-wheelbase open wagons, bound for the 'Tip' at Kirkham after clearance work on the north side of Manchester, August 1979.

Permanent way material storage – Manchester Victoria, April 1978. A smaller, but equally aged, trolley to the one in use at Ashbury's (p. 122) is seen stored amid the stacks of chairs, fishplates, sleepers and tools beneath the expanse of the A665 road bridge.

Way out

1

C.R. MASSI

A Class 40-hauled ballast train makes its way west through Edge Hill station shortly after leaving Tuebrook CE Sidings, August 1979.

Ground and shunting signals at Bridge 132, Godley Junction Sidings, May 1979. These busy sidings saw plenty of activity day and night, being the diesel/electric handover point for Fiddlers Ferry coal trains routed via Stockport Tiviot Dale – hence the Class 25 and 76 locomotives.

No. 25144 and an unidentified Class 40 bring their train of Vanfits and Cargowagons past Chester 3A signal-box and its splendid semaphore signals.

On a hot July day in 1976 a Class 40-powered
Manchester Victoria working waits time beneath
Llandudno's signal gantry.

Manchester-bound Class 310 unit no. 072 rushes past the newly ballasted Stockport Edgeley Junction, the driver confident in the knowledge that his passage is safely protected by the oil lamp-illuminated 'Banner' signals.

A Class 47-hauled bank holiday Monday (May 1979) relief working to Blackpool North passes an example of the vintage LMS multi-aspect 'Cluster' colour-light signals installed during Manchester Victoria's partial resignalling in 1929. 'Cluster' signals were first introduced by the Southern Railway at London's Blackfriars and Cannon Street stations. The unusual light configuration – red and green in the horizontal plane, yellow top and bottom vertically – was designed to placate the concerns of railway engineers. There was a belief that the loftily positioned four-aspect vertical-plane colour-light signals might not all be visible to drivers. This was subsequently proved to be unfounded and the use of 'Cluster' signals was gradually abandoned. By the time this photograph was taken Manchester Victoria was unique in still using them. In the background is Chester's Brewery – Manchester's finest purveyors of 'Best Mild' – which like much of the scene is now history. The brewery closed a long time ago and parts of the buildings have been converted into apartments.

Carlisle, May 1976. A Glasgow Central (via Dumfries) Class 45-hauled train is held at one of the station's modern multi-aspect colour-light signals, controlled by Carlisle's newly commissioned Power Box. During the early 1970s the West Coast Main Line between Warrington and Carlisle was resignalled in readiness for the introduction of through London–Glasgow electric train services on 6 May 1974. Three new Power Boxes (Warrington, Preston, Carlisle) replaced 161 manual signal-boxes and thousands of semaphore signals. The combination of modern signalling and electric motive power trimmed almost an hour off the pre-1974 London–Glasgow journey time. This initiative sadly swept away many vestiges of the LNWR and LMS. However, it did succeed in making a positive statement to the travelling public – British Rail was finally leaving its steam age past behind.

A Class 506 unit has just passed Guide Bridge Junction signal-box on its way to Manchester Piccadilly. The line branching to the left is for Stockport trains and the right-hand junction, controlled by the multi-aspect colour-light signal, is the now lifted freight only link to Ashton Moss North Junction. While the main line through Guide Bridge (the Woodhead route) boasted modern signalling, the surrounding complicated rail network remained antiquated long after the 1970s. For example, nearby Denton Junction signal-box was one of the last BR locations to use gas lighting.

A Lancashire and Yorkshire Railway signal-box awaits demolition, winter 1979.

Deganwy station crossing, July 1976. A Blaenau Ffestiniog-bound Metro Cammell two-car DMU rumbles past the signal-box controlling the wooden gates (note the wheel to open and shut the gates). In this photograph the multi-wired telegraph poles are still in use. Today the gates have been replaced by half barriers, complete with audible and visual warnings.

Astley Crossing, August 1978. A Liverpool-bound Class 108 unit flashes by, passengers and driver safely protected by the closed crossing gates. Unfortunately in later years this was the site of a fatal accident involving a train and a motor car.

Buckley Wells crossing, Bury, October 1979. The older girl is making sure the two youngsters get across safely. Their dog is also clearly aware that it is not a place to linger. This location has lost its wooden gates and wire fencing in favour of modern high-security versions. It is now amid the East Lancashire Railway's loco and carriage works complex. However, the view from the spot where this photograph was taken has changed little over the last three decades.

Opposite, top: Ex-L&Y crossing gates at Buckley Wells, July 1979. This view is looking towards Manchester with Bury Electric Depot and its resident Class 504 EMUs on the left.

Opposite, bottom: Chain-link wire fencing – Godley Junction, May 1979. In the days before the proliferation of palisade fencing a double-headed Class 76-hauled train rumbles past one of this location's many semaphore shunting signals.

Time and neglect were obviously getting the better of this sign's location. The trip hazards caused by the crumbling building, poor lighting and fading sign do not bode well for the unsuspecting railwayman.

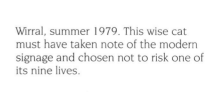

Wirral, summer 1979. This wise cat must have taken note of the modern signage and chosen not to risk one of its nine lives.

Speed restriction – Guide Bridge, winter 1975. This profiled-steel speed restriction sign, a throwback to the days of steam, does not look as if it has had a coat of paint since the smoky days of the 1960s. This type of speed restriction sign was common on BR during the 1970s and surprisingly can still be found in use on today's modernised railway.

CHAPTER SEVEN

The Enthusiast

The 1970s were a decade of great significance to the North-Western rail enthusiast. The changing face of the region's railways and society would affect enthusiast specials, preservation and train spotting. Thankfully, over the last three decades the effects have translated into the amazingly strong and multi-faceted enthusiast movement we have today.

ENTHUSIAST SPECIALS

At the start of the 1970s things appeared very bleak for the future of enthusiast specials. This was in complete contrast to the heady 1966 to 1968 'Farewell to Steam' years when well-filled enthusiast specials were very much part of the North-West rail scene – the last bastion of BR steam.

At the time steam was not allowed on the main line and the diesel/electric motive power that had replaced it was shunned by many of the mourning steam enthusiasts. How things would soon change. By the end of the 1970s steam and modern traction would be hauling specials throughout the North-West in a way not imaginable at the start of the decade. These trains would engage, foster and spawn the comprehensive railway preservation movement that was getting under way. During the decade steam was to return to the main line and reawaken interest in those enthusiasts who had thought it was all over on 11 August 1968. By the end of 1979 steam specials had become commonplace on BR-approved routes, such as the Hope Valley, Cumbrian and North Wales coastlines, and the Settle–Carlisle route.

Modern traction would find its own devoted followers. No longer would BR's post-1968 motive power be dismissed as 'Blue Boxes'. The demise of many classes of 'First Generation' locos was to trigger a return to the 1960s farewell frenzy, which would lead to the preservation of 1970s North-West stalwarts such as the Class 24 and 40.

PRESERVATION

The saving of steam locomotives (main line and industrial) was the catalyst for railway preservation. Along with enthusiasm, engineering facilities, money and skills, somewhere to keep and run them was needed. During the early years preserved lines such as the East Lancashire Railway were but a dream; redundant steam sheds provided an ideal solution, and the 1970s steam centres at Carnforth (Steamtown), Dinting and Southport motive power depots became the stepping stones to what we have today. Unfortunately, despite their popularity, which resulted from an increasingly affluent and leisure time-conscious 1970s public, only Carnforth now survives as the private base of the West Coast Railway Company. Health and Safety along with preservation progress has made them part of the North-West's railway history. Thankfully, steam locomotives were not the only focus of the preservationists' attentions. No aspect of the North-West's changing and disappearing rail scene escaped them. The only problem was that there was so much that had to be saved – 'modern' traction, rolling stock, signalling, track, buildings, station furniture, machinery and know-how – in fact, the whole infrastructure. Today this equipment forms a rich legacy provided by the foresight of those 1970s activists. There are now specialists in every aspect of old-style railway operation, making it possible for everyone to experience much of what began to disappear from the North-West rail scene during the 1970s.

A Class 40-hauled TBLS special attracts the attention of platform-end spotters at Manchester Victoria.

TRAIN SPOTTING

With its immense variety and activity, the 1970s North-West rail scene was a magnet for anyone with more than a passing interest in trains.

Train spotting, either formally using the indispensable Ian Allan *Combined Volume* to underline 'cops' or simply just watching trains, was still a popular pastime for all age groups. The bridge parapet, lineside, sheds, sidings and stations, among many other places, were regular haunts for the avid enthusiast. Compared with today's Health and Safety-conscious world it is quite amazing how freely you could wander in search of trains during the 1970s.

The pastime dates back to the nineteenth century and proved to be a great way to learn about commerce, engineering/technology and geography – all part and parcel of understanding railways. These hidden benefits, together with the sharpening of perseverance and tenacity skills in search of elusive 'cops', has been the making of many individuals.

Sadly the 1970s would witness the beginning of the end of train spotting. Subsequent decades would bring the 'anorak' stigma, paranoia, reduced variety and restrictions, which would combine to suppress its popularity. Today at 1970s spotting hotspots such as Carlisle, Crewe, Liverpool, Manchester and Preston you will be lucky to find more than one or two die-hards encamped on the platform ends. The days of duffle coats, and shoulder bags (BEA, BOAC, Inter-City or Sport) filled with tatty notepads, ham butties, soup or Oxo flasks and pop bottles are long gone.

Thankfully today, railway enthusiasm is alive and well; books, magazines, videos/DVDs, clubs/societies, enthusiast specials and preservation fill the gap left by train spotting.

The 'Western Memorial' arrives at Crewe, 29 January 1977. This special was one of a series that ran during the final weeks of the iconic Class 52 'Westerns' life on British Rail. This particular train had set out early in the morning from London Paddington and was routed via Swindon, the Severn Tunnel and Shrewsbury to Crewe. The photograph appeared in the May 1977 issue of *Railway World*.

The realisation that the Woodhead route's days were numbered triggered several specials over the route. This one was most unusual because it brought a double-headed Class 76 passenger train to Manchester Piccadilly. Since the withdrawal of the Sheffield Victoria passenger services in 1970, the Class 506 units were the only representatives of DC power at Piccadilly. On this occasion 76011 and 76025 are seen leaving the station with a packed Hertfordshire Railtours 'Trans-Pennine Freighter' on 27 October 1979.

'The Peak Express' on 15 October 1977 brought Class 44 power, no. 44004 *Great Gable*, to Manchester Piccadilly. The then fledgling Diesel and Electric Group who went on to preserve several 'First Generation' locomotives organised the special train. The 44s were the pioneer of the Peak Class 45/46; they gained their nickname because the ten 44s were named after northern peaks. There is a strong similarity with the Class 44s appearance and their ancestors, the sadly scrapped LMS diesel pioneers 10000 and 10001. It is therefore particularly fortunate that two Class 44s were preserved, as they are a link with a missing piece of Britain's railway heritage.

No. 4472 *Flying Scotsman*, having been repatriated from the USA in 1973 by Bill McAlpine, was a regular main line performer in the North-West, particularly during the later part of the 1970s. Carnforth's ex-BR motive power depot, Steamtown, also under the auspices of Sir William, became a regular haunt for the locomotive. This steam centre was very popular with enthusiasts and the general public during the 1970s. Brake van rides, a miniature railway, unrestricted access to the depot and yards, and BR's Collector's Corner (annexe to the Euston outlet) made a visit something few people could resist. The ability to relive the BR steam days in authentic surroundings is clear from this photograph.

Above: A regular 1970s main-line performer – restored Barry hulk No. 5690 *Leander* – captivates a young enthusiast at Dinting Railway Centre on 16 October 1976.

Right: A steam special stops to take on water at Earlstown.

Opposite: No. 44932 peeps out of Carnforth's reinforced concrete ex-LMS steam shed, Easter 1977. Reinforced concrete was also used for the construction of the depot's coaling tower (one of only two now left in England). Sadly this material has a tendency to 'blow' and has consigned many of the North-West's more unusual buildings to the stone crusher in recent years.

No. 6115 *Scots Guardsman* is prepared for one of its few 1970s main line turns at Dinting Railway Centre. This sub-shed of Gorton was also a popular enthusiast haunt in the 1970s, attracting many visitors over the years. It became an established base or watering hole for main-line locomotives and also home to *Bahamas*, *Blue Peter* and *Bittern*. Unfortunately, by the early 1990s it had been forced to close owing to a proposed redevelopment that never happened, and the centre's residents were dispersed throughout the UK.

A Class 40-hauled enthusiast special has just arrived at Dinting station (Woodhead route) with several hundred visitors for the adjacent Railway Centre. Attractions over the Easter 1979 weekend included No. 5305 and Midland Compound No. 1000 in steam.

Starting young – Edge Hill, summer 1979. By now the trolley-bound young spotter will be approaching thirty years old and the two chaps will be over fifty. I wonder if they remember this afternoon out and if it laid the foundations of a life-long love of railways.

One day . . . – Manchester Piccadilly, Easter 1978. Would this spotter become a driver? What did the driver of 83005 make of the situation? His facial expression prompts several possibly colourful suggestions.

In 1977 Class 31 haulage west of the Pennines was extremely unusual. The enthusiast bush telegraph must have been deployed very quickly on 9 July because this train, the delayed 13.20 from Skegness, is filled with 'gricers' taking advantage of a rare opportunity to sample 31243 haulage through to Manchester Piccadilly (the location of the photograph). Little did we know that five years later Class 31 TransPennine haulage and, unbelievably, Southern region Class 33 power on Cardiff trains to Manchester would be commonplace.

'Standing room only.' Whistler fans fill the brake section of
this Bangor-bound train, hauled by 40046, at Llandudno
Junction, summer 1979.

Ready for the off. Driver and enthusiasts prepare to depart
with a North Wales-bound working, Platform 12, Manchester
Victoria.

A spotter watches the arrival of Class 25s in tandem to collect a mixture of northbound wagons from the goods yard adjacent to Stoke-on-Trent station, winter 1978.

Even on New Year's Eve 1976 this duffel coat-clad spotter has ventured out in search of trains. Ashbury's wooden-slatted, wrought-iron benches make a comfortable but chilly place to view the regular freight and passenger activity passing through the station – far better than sitting at home watching repeats on a black-and-white television. The fashionably clad gentleman was probably heading home after working at one of the nearby heavy engineering companies. Long Christmas holidays had not been invented then.

Buffer Stop

It is hoped that this look around the 1970s northern scene, and the accompanying narrative, has been entertaining, informative, nostalgic and thought-provoking.

I've endeavoured to show that the world of railways is made up of many inter-related elements, all of which are influenced by the key driving forces of life – economics, politics, society and technology. Subjects that revolve around people, their actions and emotions. If the contents of the book have appealed to a broad spectrum of people, not just those with an avid interest in railways, it will have served its purpose and my photographic endeavours thirty years ago will have been worthwhile.

The 1970s were a significant period in the history of railways in the North-West, the culmination of changes in the world which began during and after the Second World War. Today we live in a period when the process of change is much quicker than ever before and what went before is soon forgotten. We no longer have the opportunity to mourn, savour or even notice the passing of familiar and commonplace aspects of our life – a symptom of our throw-away world perhaps? So it is more important than ever that all facets of our current rail scene are captured on film or disk for future generations to ponder, sample and study. This will also help to ensure that nostalgia does not become yet another victim of our modern way of life.

End of the Line – Bury Bolton Street station, winter 1977. A Manchester Victoria-bound Class 504 unit waits for passengers on a damp, windswept afternoon. Today the buffer stop has been removed and the line beyond reinstated to Rawtenstall. Bury Bolton Street is now a busy junction station with East Lancashire Railway trains departing east for Heywood and north along the Irwell Valley.